FASHION *IN ACTION*

A series of concise, approachable books about current, global issues around fashion, offering readers guidance on how to become active participants in its future, and acting as calls to action.

BOOKS IN THE SERIES

Slow, by Hazel Clark
Appropriation, by Benjamin Linley Wild
Failure, by Nick Rees-Roberts
Animal, by Simona Segre-Reinach

FAILURE

NICK REES-ROBERTS

BLOOMSBURY VISUAL ARTS
LONDON • NEW YORK • OXFORD • NEW DELHI • SYDNEY

BLOOMSBURY VISUAL ARTS
Bloomsbury Publishing Plc, 50 Bedford Square, London, WC1B 3DP, UK
Bloomsbury Publishing Inc, 1359 Broadway, New York, NY 10018, USA
Bloomsbury Publishing Ireland, 29 Earlsfort Terrace, Dublin 2, D02 AY28, Ireland

BLOOMSBURY, BLOOMSBURY VISUAL ARTS and the Diana logo
are trademarks of Bloomsbury Publishing Plc

First published in Great Britain 2026

Series design: Adriana Brioso
Cover images: Andrej Lišakov/Unsplash

A catalogue record for this book is available from the British Library.

A catalog record for this book is available from the Library of Congress.

ISBN: PB: 978-1-3503-6997-9
ePDF: 978-1-3503-6998-6
eBook: 978-1-3503-6999-3

Typeset by Integra Software Services Pvt. Ltd.
Printed and bound in India

For product safety related questions contact productsafety@bloomsbury.com.

To find out more about our authors and books visit www.bloomsbury.com
and sign up for our newsletters.

CONTENTS

SERIES EDITORS' PREFACE

Fashion In Action responds directly to the upsurge of interest in critical issues in fashion—the industry, its ethics, its values, its contribution to global profits, its challenges amidst profound planetary change. When we choose what to wear, the connections we make might be understood as a chapter in a larger global fashion story. How do we re-imagine fashion as participants, encouraging a "freedom of thinking", while unraveling the past, challenging our present, and pointing to the future? This series goes beyond delineating global trends and fashion practices to imagine the very concepts of fashion anew. After all, we are planetary subjects in the making.

In a world seemingly full of disruptions, what do we make of failure? If fashion could somehow unpack its own existence as an arbiter of ascension and success, we might then embrace the imperfections often required to create and imagine anything worthwhile. In *Failure*, Nick Rees-Roberts argues that this critical tool for understanding our tastes, judgements, and cultural standards that shift alongside fashion, has long remained omitted or overlooked even though essential to the creative process. Failure just is, the author writes. And it has the potential to teach us about ourselves and the structures of an industry many perceive as failing our planet. Perhaps, this book suggests, fashion just needs to fail. Narratives depicting a rise and fall, especially the ones we read about in headlines, erase the powerful role of social networks and even the paradigm of global fashion capitalism. Fashion can turn on us at any time, this book reminds us, especially when failure remains relegated to the margins.

Each book in this series is divided into three parts and a Call to Action. In "Failure Mode," we read that failure is commonplace as a part of the creative process. To invert a paradigm that has long influenced how we perceive fashion and its countercultures, failure emerges as an important critical tool with which to re-evaluate—envision us failing again and again, so challenging and yet essential—as we assess the new. Social, political, and economic factors, among others, create the losses that are somehow deemed as going wrong. From hungry consumers of digital content to an industry that markets obsessively auras of perfection and success as synonyms for modernity, this book challenges us to consider whether or not fashion even works anymore. Simply put, for whom and for what purposes has fashion and its collapses even existed? Turning to cultural theorists like Elizabeth Wilson to understand the notion of refashioning the old and daring to be ugly with the new, and to fashion campaigns gone devastatingly awry, this section reflects on the darker sides of omission and deception that inhabit a deeply emotional zone. Failure as a "creative motor", the author writes, unmakes and re-imagines a process through which we learn about ourselves and the shortcomings of the power structures we inhabit. To entice change and counteract deep, collective fears, fashion must fail.

"Aesthetics of Failure" analyzes the obsolescent layers of fast fashion and its betrayal of the body and self. From Honoré de Balzac's fictional representations to the Fugly and Weirdcore, fashion is subject to a kind of layering process that, once deconstructed, imagines how we define its conventional norms. How we re-imagine failure and fashion, then, depends on what we make of the fall from prominence. Here the author channels Giorgio Agamben, wondering if fashion failure might reside somewhere in between the "not yet" and "no more". How might we understand more fully the incongruences in our midst, from things like period costumes at a gas station to the now iconic pigeon clutch purse in *Sex and the City*? Reputability, this book reminds us, trumps the aesthetics of failure. And remembering Susan Sontag, the author also ponders at which precise point something vulgar, campy or kitschy might be so beyond the pale that it becomes really, really good.

In "Fame and Failure", the author reflects on it all and finds a world full of: Falls. Obsessions. Hemlines. Scandal. Shame. With a nod to our own fashion literacy of couturiers and designer celebrities, we witness and replay complex situations almost cinematographically, as if to anticipate the tidy threads of demise. This section points to unleashing the potential of failure in order to "re-position creativity" within fashion. Failure becomes not just a point of reflection, but an important critical tool for *Fashion In Action*.

The Call to Action is like a prism through which we might gain insight and assume collaborative roles in our re-thinking of failure. It is no longer feasible to sustain creation for creation's sake, but a wisdom that might better inform our choices and design exercises. Re-thinking *Failure*, the author writes, implies asking us to dream the impossible and initiate the possible, and challenge basic assumptions. What are we waiting for?

Regina A. Root and Hazel Clark

PREFACE

Failure

1.a A failing to occur, be performed, or be produced; an omitting to perform something due or required; default.

1.b. † A lapse, a slight fault; a failing, infirmity. *Obsolete*.

2. The fact of becoming exhausted or running short, giving way under trial, breaking down in health, declining in strength or activity, etc.

3.a. The fact of failing to effect one's purpose; want of success; an instance of this.

3.b. *concrete*. A thing or person that proves unsuccessful.

4. The fact of failing in business; bankruptcy, insolvency.

(Oxford English Dictionary, revised second edition)

Failure is central to fashion. This counter-intuitive claim is the starting point for an inquiry into a concept not ordinarily associated with the world of adornment, style, beauty, and dress. Fashion thrives on the promotion of fame and success, integrated as it is into the structure and logic of consumer capitalism. However, beneath all the hype and luster, fashion also has a history of failure. Taking examples of designers and brands from across the world, I deploy failure as a critical tool to rethink fashion and its intensive globalized system of production, distribution, consumption, and representation. Drawing on a wide range of sources including literary, journalistic, and philosophical texts, as well as many contemporary films and TV series, this book considers the fundamental role of failure in the evolution of the fashion system.

The links between dress and success are hardwired into our culture. In the late 1960s, famous Hollywood costume designer Edith Head, the winner of no less than eight Academy Awards, who had dressed such stars as Grace Kelly and Audrey Hepburn, published her tidbits of advice in a book co-written with Joe Hyams called *How to Dress for Success*.[1] The goal was to instruct readers on how to look younger, prettier, and slimmer if they wanted to attract and keep a man, get a better job, earn more money, enable their husbands to move up the ladder of success and widen their circle of friends and so forth. Seen from the perspective of the twenty-first century, this quaint guide to social climbing through managing appearance is a precursor to our own shame-inducing make-over reality shows that similarly manipulate style, fashion, and dress as discursive instruments of control, as the prescriptive means to discipline consumers through a normative biopolitics of identity (of class, race, gender, sexuality, and the body). Like John T. Molloy's 1975 volume, similarly titled *Dress for Success*,[2] which first popularized the concept of power dressing, these aspirational pearls of wisdom indicate that failing to dress appropriately—to respect the codification of the fashion industry—has historically been mapped onto other manifestations of deficiency, decline, breakdown, and collapse (be they structural or individual, socio-economic or psychological). The traditional conflation of personal appearance with professional achievement also evokes the troubling specter of embarrassment and shame routinely associated with the negativity of failure—an inherent part of an increasingly distorting and dysfunctional consumer capitalism.

Before we take a deep dive into failure in the specific context of the fashion sector, a few words first on the background to the inception of this book. For many queer people, feelings of embarrassment and shame associated with identity also relate—at an unconscious level—to how we experience success and failure. With the benefit of hindsight, I realize that writing this book may simply have been a way to deal with some of those personal insecurities—to manage the fear of failure and the residue of shame—by displacing them through the orthodox mode of speculation that is academic writing. Some recent professional setbacks also led me to wrestle concurrently with the problem of how as individuals we process the negative feelings of disappointment, frustration, and inertia associated with the specific organizational forms of failure.

I first thought about the topic in relation to fashion when I attended the International Festival of Fashion, Photography, and Accessories at Hyères in the south of France in April 2019. During a panel on fashion entrepreneurship, discussing the economic models for emerging labels, Nicolas Santi-Weil, the CEO of AMI Paris, described how in the world of Paris fashion, designers are not allowed to fail, or at least not permitted to acknowledge failure as part and parcel of their experience of working in the creative industries. Also on the panel, designer Stéphanie Coudert, who having won a prize at the festival in 1999 had gone on to launch her label, described how her vocation—her creative will to design—had been subsumed into the financial need to head up a brand and manage an expanding business through a traditional model of global distribution. Bigger is better, according to the capitalist logic of economic growth. By taking the brave step to downscale her business focusing on the fabrication of semi-bespoke garments, Coudert later evoked her designs as the production of silent clothing, thereby positioning her work off-grid or outside the dominant framework of branding, promotion, and celebrity laid down by the fashion industry. However, keeping a small, independent couture house afloat nowadays is tougher than ever: in 2024 she finally called it a day, shuttered Maison Coudert, put her business into receivership and accepted a position as a dressmaker within the Christian Dior Couture atelier. What had struck me, listening to the panel discussion back in 2019, was how frankly Coudert addressed the question of failure in the fashion business and how difficult it is for creatives to acknowledge and deal with this inevitable part of their working lives. My endeavor to write a book on the subject was derailed a year later by the Covid-19 pandemic, a sea-change on so many levels. One thing it did was to spotlight and call into question the hollow imperatives of ambition and achievement that shape the capitalist discourses of business motivation and self-improvement—those injunctions to ascension, fame, and success that animate commercial culture and drive creative activity.

One of the main points of this book is precisely to argue that in the context of the fashion business, failure is a widespread and common occurrence, as indeed it is elsewhere in the creative industries and artistic sectors. Commercial failure, in particular, might not therefore simply be a source of personal embarrassment, despite often being seen as the individual's fault. Failure is thus often put down to a lack of talent, ambition, motivation, or inspiration rather than the shortcomings of capitalism—the structural constraints, economic variables, and material parameters of an integrated globalized system like fashion. The intended message of the book is therefore that a critical focus on failure might indeed inspire change.

On a more macro level, the book also offers a series of reflections on the fashion industry's need to fail due to wider issues of sustainability, inequality, and exploitation. Writing about a heavily marketing-driven business culture like fashion is difficult without reproducing the promotional language of ambition, aspiration, and wish-fulfilment, a mythology that promotes branded image, fame, and success as the key goals of design rather than focusing on more productive forms of creative transmission, regeneration, and renewal. Of course, this is changing generationally, a point raised by the Apple TV mini-series *La Maison* (2024), in which the old guard of patrician couturiers and corporate behemoths is challenged by the emergence of a new generation of digital-native designers with an opposing ecological agenda of sustainability and cultural ideology of inclusivity.

Indeed, there are others ways of writing about creativity and commerce than through the lens of corporate marketing and promotion: this book might therefore also contribute to the existing critical literature of consumer culture through its alternative, oppositional coverage of the business of fashion. As we shall see, consumer capitalism is in a state of chronic crisis; it has in effect gone into failure mode. Another question raised here is therefore whether the fashion industry functions properly anymore—whether it even works. Failure might therefore be the suitable prism through which to write a revised negative history of fashion.

1
FAILURE MODE

An account of failure in fashion may as well begin on the catwalk. In 1993, super-model Naomi Campbell fell during designer Vivienne Westwood's ready-to-wear Autumn/Winter show. Wearing impossibly high platform heels, Campbell fell to the ground before smiling and getting back up to continue down the runway. Her fall garnered intense media scrutiny, which only intensified in the years that followed as she became a global celebrity and one of the fashion industry's most enduring super-models. The monographic exhibition of her career at the V&A museum in London in 2024 included reference to the model's fall as an integral part of her renown: "That fall is part of me," she is quoted as saying, "so I own the fall, it's ok, people make mistakes. The most important thing for me is just getting up and doing it again."[1] This mishap, however anecdotal, draws our attention to the physical embodiment of success and failure: rising and succeeding, falling and failing, getting back up and continuing, or instead choosing to give up and move on. The catwalk pratfall is thus merely the spectacular tip of the iceberg. I am thinking here about failure more conceptually as a negative ethos in the overlapping but discrete disciplinary contexts of fashion design (the history of designer-branded clothing) and creative industries (in particular, the ethical and cultural critiques of the global fashion ecosystem).

My concern is to unravel the interrelationship between forms of individual and collective failure—both creative and commercial—in the context of fashion. So, by fails, I do not simply mean wardrobe malfunctions, runway mishaps, or design glitches; rather, the aim is to problematize the whole notion of failure and to map out the contexts

FIGURE 1 Model Naomi Campbell trips on the runway at the Vivienne Westwood Fall 1993 RTW show.

of its iteration by focusing on the histories of designers (their houses, labels, and brands) within specific commercial contexts. A focus on failure might therefore be a way of contesting the fixation with fame, ambition, and recognition that structures popular representations of the fashion industry.

In its place, I profile a number of designers whose stories have either been widely documented by the film and media industries or else overlooked because they have not followed the normative route towards visibility and celebrity set out by the fashion industry that counts as success. One of my incentives for this study is sociologist Tim Edwards' comment that "the academic world of fashion often has little to say about designer labels, no real perspective or point of view."[2] Through a preference for single-author studies, he notes that "most fashion historians remain more enraptured by the power of design than by the commercial significance of the label per se."[3] Indeed, failure in fashion, in its most immediate sense (evoking as it does feelings of embarrassment, disappointment, or shame) is, in essence, about the business fail—at the most fundamental level, the failure to sell product. In the current conjuncture, survival for an emerging designer label is particularly tough due to factors that include the demise of wholesale and the end of the e-commerce boom with the downfall of a number of luxury e-tailers; a packed retail market in which consumers are over-stimulated by the endless choice of brands and labels on offer; not to mention wider issues of financial and geopolitical instability (for example, the impact of Brexit in the UK or the effects of the Chinese economic downturn on global consumption).

I am thereby mobilizing failure here as a way of undoing the fault lines of an industry over-invested in the rhetorical promotion of permanent success (articulated as an over-investment in commercial growth, individual attainment, and aesthetic perfection) in which no one can afford to fail or, at the very least, be seen to fail. However, failure in fashion surely must mean more than simply failing to sell product, however fundamental the financial bottom line is to fashion as an industry. With that in mind, this book therefore balances individual histories of creative and commercial failure in design with a focus on the collective setbacks, aesthetic imperfections, and structural breakdown of the traditional fashion system. The broader ambition is to examine the different categories for thinking about failure in fashion—balancing both the aesthetic and commercial faces of design.

By focusing on the workings of the twenty-first-century fashion system, I am situating the paradigm of success and failure within the current breakdown of many of the traditional structures, practices, and thinking of the global industry. Lately, fashion has been seen by many as a failing industry—a dirty word used to symbolize the ethical wrongs of ecological meltdown, industrial pollution, global inequalities, and mindless materialism. In May 2024, *The Guardian* even devoted an editorial to the demise of the independent designer label The Vampire's Wife, viewed as both a jolt to the system and a worrying sign of the times for the vitality of independent brands following the collapse earlier that year of the e-commerce platform and online wholesaler Matches. The business had started out as a suburban bricks-and-mortar store, later expanding and introducing international luxury brands to the UK market, launching its e-commerce site in 2006 before being sold to private equity investors for some 800 million pounds in 2017. This demise of independent labels and e-commerce platforms stands in stark contrast to the continued acceleration of ultra-fast fashion with the rise of third-generation brands such as Chinese market-leaders Shein and Temu targeting Gen Z (following the original heavyweights Zara and H&M and the digital-first models of ASOS and Boohoo) with their ecologically unsustainable business model of low-priced, data-driven, Tik-Tok-friendly, carbon-heavy, disposable products.

Amidst this hyper-production, toxic waste, and ecological meltdown, fashion still notoriously idealizes perfection. In his filmed documentary portrait of his mother, Franca Sozzani, the influential fashion journalist and former editor-in-chief of *Vogue Italia*, entitled *Franca: Chaos and Creation* (2016), Francesco Carrozzini leads his interview with the following question: have you ever failed? Reclining pensively in her car, the subject replies that naturally everyone fails and that it's an impossible question to answer; if you think you never fail, you think you're perfect, Sozzani replies.

By locating failure (and its adjacent categories of imperfection, mishap, glitch, disappointment, demise, breakdown, and collapse) at the negative core of fashion, we might therefore start to undo the industry's commercial narratives and imperatives of perfection, glamor, and success.

Take the example of Kim Jones, menswear designer at Christian Dior from 2018 to 2025, the jewel in the crown of the LVMH luxury group. An interview in *The Guardian* in 2019 reiterated the discourse of achievement-based culture by presenting Jones as at once an anomaly and a success story. With a modest following on Instagram, he is not a celebrity as such but nonetheless has a certain influence. In the interview he is quoted as saying: "I'm very fast. Being indecisive is an awful thing and shows a weakness of character. You need to know what you like … These jobs are not an easy ride … I have worked and sacrificed for it."[4] Underpinning the corporate hyperbole of drive and ambition is the reliance on a self-conscious or self-promotional performance of neoliberal rationalization: the designer is thereby singled out to represent growth, efficiency, and optimization. Failing to attain perfection is not something Jones appears to worry about, at least not publicly.

However, the specter of failure, and its attendant affective negativity, looms large in other instances. Take a feature published in *The New York Times* in 2018 exploring "How Marc Jacobs Fell Out of Fashion."[5] Falling (as in "from grace" or "flat on one's face") is commonly used as an anxiety-inducing image to invoke failure. Moreover, the dynamics of ascension (rising, climbing) and descent (falling, collapsing) are routine rhetorical features in representations of success and failure; and images of vertical movement (up and down) recur throughout this study. One might in passing take as symptomatic the titles of the following books to illustrate fashion's focus on ascent and descent: street photographer Bill Cunningham's memoir, *Fashion Climbing* and author Alicia Drake's account of designers in 1970s Paris, *The*

Beautiful Fall.[6] The *Times* piece on Marc Jacobs "falling out of fashion" speculated on the reasons for the designer's decline since leaving his position as creative director at Louis Vuitton in 2013 and the devaluation of his own label, drawing on the conventional rise and fall narrative: the designer was seen as out of touch in a saturated market; his vision no longer coincided with the zeitgeist. Rewind a decade and you notice the very different language used to discuss the effect Jacobs had on the New York scene: reporting on a show in 2007, journalist Guy Trebay satirically captured the designer's aura. His buzzy runway shows were depicted as a who's who of celebrity culture of the period and the incarnation of downtown cool of the decade.[7]

Success and Failure: Loaded Words

As you read further, I invite you to keep in mind the following questions:

1 Why do fashion houses shut and labels and brands go out of business?
2 Why do designers choose to leave the industry?
3 Why do some rising stars, celebrated and promoted early in their careers, fall or even fail to take off?
4 How do designers negotiate and manage success and failure over the course of a career?

These overarching questions might encourage us to think about the overlaps and divergences between the different forms of creative and commercial failure that are rooted in the discourse of neoliberal rationalization. In an image-obsessed industry such as fashion, driven by the promotional imperatives of marketing and branding, in which "[n]o venture is ever a failure," in which designers rarely "speak candidly about their work in a market where they are not only artists, but also peddlers of a product,"[8] the story of the (more often male) designer's success, conveyed through the public image of its subject, is a particularly potent one. In her editorial to the special issue on failure for the journal *Vestoj*, Anja Aronowsky Cronberg comments that in the fashion industry "a downfall is transformed into a temporary glitch in the machinery, and a breakdown is nothing but an occasion to rise again, like a phoenix from the ashes."[9]

Success and Failure. Two "loaded words" according to literary critic Marjorie Garber, who contends that all such terms are inherently weighted, carrying with them the alternatives, even opposites, which lie below the surface to produce a paradoxical tension.[10] To start with failure: the term derives from the Middle English *failen*, borrowed from Anglo-Norman *faillir*, from Vulgar Latin *fallire*, an alteration of Latin *fallere*, meaning to deceive or to disappoint. Alternative roots are to be found in the Proto-Indo-European for to lie, to deceive, or to stumble. Following the post-structuralist philosopher Jacques Derrida's interpretative model of deconstruction that mapped out crucial binary oppositions "to show how these terms are inscribed within a systematic structure of hierarchical privilege, such that one of each pair will always appear to occupy the sovereign or governing position,"[11] attention to the category of failure—to stumbling, slipping up, deceiving, or disappointing, iterations of which might appear out of context or out of place—invariably sheds light on the structure underpinning a whole normative value system in which, following Derrida's lead, the subordinate term "has an equal (maybe a prior) claim to be treated as a condition of possibility for the entire system."[12]

At the outset, one might well ask how to dispense with a paradigm shaped by the opposition of two terms, a framework that seems to structure our collective understanding and infiltrate our inner feelings of what it means to succeed and to fail. The *Neutral* was precisely semiologist Roland Barthes' attempt to go beyond the prescriptive binary regime of the either/or that frames the epistemology of success and failure. To outplay the normative paradigm of success and failure also involved the author's own re-appraisal of his earlier writings. Despite good patches, each book is exposed upon rereading to

Barthes' sense of inevitable failure. Linking success/failure to sexuality, he posits shame or disgrace as a possibly productive third category.[13] In place of the either/or, Barthes proposed the neutral as a reading of the regime of the "neither/nor" as a rejection of binary thinking: "I define the Neutral as that which outplays the paradigm, or rather I call Neutral everything that baffles the paradigm."[14] Meaning is accordingly generated by conflict; to choose one term over the other is invariably to sacrifice meaning. Let us keep in mind the postulate of the *neither/nor* as a way of liberating fashion from the shackles of success and failure—something that is ever harder for us to imagine, given a society obsessed with competition, hollowed out by neoliberal rationalization and deregulation, and manipulated by digital algorithms.

One of the reasons I turn to Barthes is the desire to flesh out, albeit speculatively, a critical alternative to this status quo. The same goes for the late literary theorist and queer thinker, Leo Bersani, whose book on Beckett, Rothko and Resnais, *Arts of Impoverishment*, co-written with Ulysse Dutoit in 1993, opened with the following provocative statement: "Surely nothing is more dangerous for an artist, or for a critic, than to be obsessed with failure,"[15] a caution that has lodged in my mind while writing this book. Bersani was asked in interview about the importance of failure to his writing and on one occasion the exchange began by mapping out his distinguished academic trajectory through the topic of failure.[16] Bersani was clearly not interested in a facile identification with instances of bad art. Likewise, I am not interested here in policing the aesthetics of "good" or "bad" fashion as such or compiling a personal list of fashion fails. Whilst one might naturally take issue with Bersani's prediiection for artists (writers, painters, or filmmakers) taken from the established Western aesthetic canon, his interest in failure is nonetheless productive. The artists that interested him were those who "were failing with respect to certain traditions and expectations connected to the mediums in which they were working and that to a certain extent this inhibits a kind of appropriation of the work which we tend, as a result of a great deal of quite effective cultural training, to take for granted."[17]

In a similar vein, success is etymologically linked to both tradition and transmission—to the word succession, which derives from the Latin *successus* from the verb *succedere*, meaning to come close after. Succeeding is, one way or another, about following rather than contesting creative norms, industry practices, or canon formations. In the context of designer fashion branding, the question of success/-ion is indexed to the media fabrication of aura and personality. It is particularly challenging for designers who take on the mantle from a high-profile founder of a fashion house: how to replace designers whose aura (their fame and charisma) is, in the public's eye, invariably tied to their label, as was the case, for example, for Peter Hawkings, who survived less than a year as Tom Ford's successor and quit abruptly in 2024.

In the context of pop culture, the link between these two terms—success and succession—might also go to explain the adoption of the so-called "quiet luxury" style of Jesse Armstrong's hit TV series for HBO, *Succession*, in the early 2020s. Michelle Matland's costume

FIGURE 2 The padded gilet as corporate uniform: still of actor Matthew Macfadyen in *Succession*.

FIGURE 3 Fashion and class shaming: the appearance of the "ludicrously capacious" Burberry bag in *Succession*.

designs promoted the aesthetic ideals of stealth wealth through the emblematic display of knitwear and caps by extremely expensive Italian luxury brands such as Loro Piana and Brunello Cucinelli. The appearance of the normcore men's gilet (also known as the finance bro vest) signaled the rise of bland corporate uniformity as a manifestation of white male privilege. In the final season screened in 2023, a socially aspirational guest is shamed at a party for her failure to adopt the sartorial codes of the milieu of ultra-rich media moguls that she has infiltrated. Her outsized Burberry monogram bag is viciously derided as "ludicrously capacious," the "monstrous" excess baggage an embarrassing token of her failed class intrusion. In short, sartorial failure—at least in this corporate milieu—means being vulgarly out of place and socially out of your depth.

Following Bersani's lead, one of the important threads of my inquiry here also involves spotlighting designers who "fail" with respect to certain traditions and expectations within the industry, the apparatus of individual economic success that includes public and corporate-sponsored prizes attributed to designers such as the LVMH, the CFDA (Council of Fashion Designers of America), or the ANDAM (*Association nationale pour le développement des arts de la mode*) prizes. Not everyone aspires to become the next success story, the next Alexandre Mattiussi, for example, whose brand AMI Paris, launched in 2011, has rapidly expanded, having secured investment from Sequoia Capital China in 2021. The brand was one of the many integrated into the Netflix series *Emily in Paris* (an elaborate case of embedded promotion) making an extended narrative appearance in season four at the French tennis tournament Roland-Garros and thereby referencing the label's own sports partnerships. With an estimated annual financial turnover of some fifty million euros, industry press reports of the brand's expansion invariably reproduce the neoliberal economic mantra of permanent growth, ambition, and strength measured solely by the label's global imprint.[18]

How, then, to reset fashion beyond the either/or logic of branded success and failure? Notwithstanding the more subversive or anti-capitalist potential of a critical understanding of failure in design, it

FIGURE 4 Advanced brand integration in the era of streaming: AMI featuring in *Emily in Paris*.

nonetheless remains challenging to think about fashion from a negative perspective (however urgent the ecological need to position reduction at the center of both industry analysis and conceptual thinking about fashion) given the overwhelming promotion of values of productivity, excess, and positivity within the industry, media, and culture. Not to mention the constant recuperation of an ethical standpoint on fashion by social media's post-ironic transformation of critique into an aestheticized concept or marketing tool, into a gimmick—the viral trend for "underconsumption-core" is a perfect illustration of this formal pattern of digital aestheticization.

Failure Narratives

The proliferation of aspirational reality TV shows on designing and modeling (from *Making the Cut* and *Next in Fashion* to *America's Next Top Model* and *Project Runway*) are clearly invested in success and failure in how they intersect with (and performatively rearticulate) powerful social indicators of image, fame, status, and wealth. The design format shows came in the wake of the repugnant spectacle of professional and personal humiliation that was *The Apprentice* (2004–17), quite clearly an ideological incubator for one man's political ambitions of megalomania and authoritarianism. Despite their ethos of caring and sharing, influenced as much as anything by the female and queer-centricity of the contestants and the audience, these design shows nonetheless stage failure by narrowly defining what it means or "what it takes" to become a successful creative in the purely economic terms of market competition: after all, "you're not making the cut" is just polite fashion-speak for "you're fired."

Furthermore, the critical question of success and failure in fashion is not simply a matter of representation for a corps of high-profile (predominantly male) designers in corporate fashion, whose lack of diversity has been vehemently called out on both legacy and social media in the early 2020s. The ways in which gender intersects with the doxa of success are often contradictory: take the first book by successful French YouTuber, influencer, and media personality, Léna Mahfouf (known under the name of Lena Situations, the first French influencer to be invited to the Met Gala in 2022), a quirky personal development/self-motivational memoir titled *Toujours Plus* (*Always More*). She is an illustration of how the new fashion entertainment—the intersection of tech with luxury—is indexed to intensified datafication and the relentless production of monetized content, the quantifiable logic for which is more is more. Mahfouf also posted a video in 2023 explaining how the launch of her concept store and lifestyle brand, Hôtel Mahfouf, had been a flop, thereby openly sharing her experience of failure with her followers.[19]

Popular profiles of the personalities of fashion further demonstrate how gender inflects appraisals of success and failure: journalist Marisa Meltzer's book about the founder and CEO of online beauty brand Glossier, Emily Weiss, focuses on its subject's ingenuity and ambition in capturing consumer attention through the rise of the "clean girl" myth through the 2010s and the brand's subsequent unsuccessful make-up launch followed by what marketers call a "vibe shift" in the early 2020s as the pretty pink products and the branded discourse of realness began to appear contrived. The publicized fall of the #girlboss phenomenon of successful female CEOs being taken down on social media was a way of containing displays of female ambition by positioning it as out-of-style. The flaw in Weiss' projected image of self-invention was that it only made room for one story, that of success. "These women who were raised up as leaders were often young and inexperienced when they took on so much responsibility, which makes a great narrative, but what's the narrative for those who failed?" Meltzer wonders.[20]

Autobiographical narratives penned by designers likewise often reiterate the well-rehearsed script of self-motivation by telling their stories of resilience and self-confidence building, and painting the designer as an emblem of capitalist success.[21] However, one might on the contrary want to rethink fashion by inhabiting the negative. The inherent risk here is of reproducing a position of privilege in relation to failure by celebrating it naively or by reinstating the language and codes of the artistic avant-garde as the yardstick by which to measure it—writer and dramatist Samuel Beckett's maxim ("Ever tried. Ever failed. No matter. Try Again. Fail Again. Fail Better"[22]) has become something of a motto in critical appraisals of failure. Not all creatives share this vision, however: the much lauded Japanese designer Yohji Yamamoto has often been cited as not only a lasting influence on the templates of Western fashion but also as a critical counter-model in an age of hyper-modern celebrity-driven marketing, leading one reporter to ask whether he might even be able to save fashion from itself.[23] In an address to the Oxford University Union in April 2018, Yamamoto described his start in fashion in Tokyo in the 1970s, where his aesthetic was considered strange, his looks read as failures, redolent of the postwar aesthetic of ruin and collapse. In his memoir, *My Dear Bomb*, published in 2010, Yamamoto posited reduction as a general philosophy of style, thereby situating his designs in the artistic legacy of modernism while paradoxically also rejecting the standard labels of avant-garde, conceptual, or anti-fashion often used to describe his work. Indeed, it is a critical commonplace to interpret Yamamoto's designs through a high-modernist lens of abstraction (the focus on his asymmetrical silhouettes, monochromatic palettes, working mostly with black), a re-composition of forms (garments with frayed edges, holes, and tears) and a type of luxurious austerity, similar to the anti-redemptive "arts of impoverishment" formulated by Bersani and Dutoit that seek to challenge and unnerve us. Citing examples of failed fashion in types of ostentation and over-grooming, the designer talks of an inherent ambivalence in fashion aesthetics between refinement and vulgarity, subtlety and frivolousness.[24]

In his Oxford Union address, Yamamoto also claimed that big-branded design and mass-produced fast fashion had "broken" fashion—indeed, the uniformization of clothing design through mass retail, characterized by normcore and the global rise of the brand Uniqlo, for example, might further suggest the generalized failure of fashion as a popular form of individual aesthetic self-expression. However, Yamamoto's own position as a high-end conceptual designer, known also to co-brand with sportswear giant Adidas on the more commercial line Y-3, points to the inbuilt contradictions involved in any discussion of the interconnections between art and commerce in contemporary fashion. Attention to the paradoxes and ambivalences inherent in fashion would therefore indicate a productive dialogue with the cultural and theoretical legacy of Marxism, in particular the renewal of interest in the writings of philosopher and critical theorist, Theodor Adorno, on the subject of such negative aesthetic categories as ugliness and kitsch, which together with camp and vulgar are discussed further in the context of fashion's post-digital imagery of failure.

In parallel, we might also consider insights from contemporary critical design thinking that seeks to embrace negative affect and space.[25] Adapting the thesis of her earlier book about rethinking the values of productivity and achievement to the arena of design, American artist Jenny Odell imagines a new vision of design that "seeks not necessarily to construct, abstract, or replace, but that responds to the present with the tools of the present. Design that accepts the existence of the world as it is, in all of its beautiful and terrible detail."[26] This negative space, Odell avers, not only involves forging new political alliances in reaction to global economic and ecological injustice (the example of an exploitative, delocalized fashion and textile industry is an obvious case in point) but also the larger project of rethinking design as less preoccupied with making than with unmaking. Her suggestive notion of "manifest dismantling," a perversion of the nineteenth-century U.S. doctrine of Manifest Destiny, is articulated as "a form of purpose bound up with remediation, something that requires us to give up the idea that progress can only face forward blindly."[27]

To reject the socio-economic determinism of forward progress and the corporate narratives of ascent and inevitable fall might therefore correlate to adopting something like gender theorist Jack Halberstam's idea of the queer art of failure to the context of fashion.[28] To embrace the negative would therefore involve a more complex conceptual understanding of the multiple and contradictory meanings of failure as a creative motor in the contemporary practices of fashion. To point the way, I provide readers with a brief map for thinking about and through failure with a contextual appraisal of related methodologies in failure studies within not only the history of the fashion business but also more broadly across the spectrum of the arts and humanities: from aesthetics, architecture, cultural studies, and literature to media arts and technologies, performance studies, philosophy, and social history.[29] These multifarious perspectives converge to posit failure as a critical tool that is not simply the privileged domain of negative affect (evoking feelings of shame, disappointment, or powerlessness) but also as potentially productive (it demands rethinking and regrouping), creative (it facilitates the emergence of new forms), nonconformist (it offers an escape from the expectations and cycles of success and achievement), structuring (it sets limits to the linear pursuit of progress and accomplishment), and transformative (it recasts the goals or outcomes of a project).[30]

Despite these many different critical framings of failure, we still live in a heavily success-driven culture in which it is still considered a dirty word. Success today in the creative industries is often reductively measured by data analysis and the combination of optimization, growth, and virality. Creatives and practitioners clearly tend to become increasingly risk averse for economic reasons. However, according to a truism in the history of technological invention, failure is essential to producing new ideas and new forms of knowledge. In other words, there is no structural change without failure, and experimentation is the key to innovation. The fear of negative judgment and the appraisal of others compounds the material consequences of failure, according to essayist Alain de Botton, who in a discussion of status anxiety explains (with a certain exaggeration) that failure can unleash a feeling of humiliation, "a corroding awareness that we have been unable to convince the world of our value and are henceforth condemned to consider the successful with bitterness and ourselves with shame."[31] According to iterations of positivist economic and cultural thought, often popularized through the rhetoric of marketing or popular psychology, while failure is often primarily internalized negatively as disappointment or shame, it can also function as a motivational force for self-learning and self-improvement.[32] However, rather than follow the coordinates of this type of inquiry, in the chapters that follow I endeavor to focus more specifically on the aesthetic forms of failure in fashion design, on the individual narratives and trajectories of designers themselves, and on instances of creative mishaps or design glitches, with a view to locating failure as a leading critical thread within a revised history of fashion. Before we get to the aesthetics and narratives of design failure, first there is the question of the breakdown of the fashion system itself to consider.

System Failure

Fashion needs to fail. This seemingly paradoxical sentiment has been voiced by a number of recent initiatives launched by actors in the industry to question the structures and imperatives of the fashion system. The 2021 and 2022 editions of *The State of Fashion*, the annual report financed by *The Business of Fashion* and *McKinsey & Company*, focused on uneven global recovery, logistical gridlock, and diminished demand in the post-Covid-19 economic context. In 2020, the collective *#rewiringfashion* sought to bring together a growing group of founding signatories including independent designers and brands (such as Altuzarra, AMI Paris, Craig Green, Erdem, Haider Ackermann, Isabel Marant), CEOs, and retailers (from Lane Crawford to Selfridges & Co) to reconfigure the fashion system, in particular its outmoded format and temporality of display. Aiming to adjust the seasonality of fashion, to reset its calendar and reimagine its modes of presentation, the proposal consolidated a previous initiative, a forum launched by Belgian designer Dries Van Noten in 2020, framed as an open letter to the industry aiming to simplify the business of fashion by making it more environmentally and socially sustainable. These initiatives formed part of a larger call to action for the industry to rethink its priorities and update its operating system without espousing the more subversive rhetoric of the anarchist *Fashion Revolution* movement, founded in 2013, the largest global activist movement geared to a more radical overhaul and collapse of the consumer system.

How, then, to interpret this recent proliferation of manifestos and movements that seek either to modify or to reconfigure a creative economy fashioned around over-production and over-consumption? Is it possible to reconcile fashion with a post-capitalist discourse that brings the structure to the point of collapse (in the vein of the *Anarchitecture Group* in New York in the 1970s, which sought to articulate a critique of the modernist impulses of contemporary culture within which the built environment was perceived as a potent symbol of our culture's worst excesses)? How to divest fashion of its systemic failings? In the global move away from individual possession (fashionable clothing conceived solely in terms of material acquisition) as the core of consumer culture, is the failure of fashion now more a necessity than a radical aspiration?

As I mentioned previously, rather than focus so much on manufacture and production, on doing and making, shouldn't we rather be focusing on undoing and remaking the idea and ideals of fashion to generate a more radical counter-discourse?[33]

To cite the work of one scholar in the fast-growing academic field of fashion sustainability studies, Kate Fletcher's research has, in my view, been central for inviting us to rethink fashion beyond the "natural" framework of consumption, drawing attention to how consumer culture conditions our experience of clothing at every level but also creates "an illusion … of clothing without use."[34] Calling for a disruptive system change in fashion thinking, a change in perspective in how we use and reuse clothing, Fletcher's redefinition of fashion post-growth constitutes a major intervention by arguing for the craft of use "to favour the practices of garment use as much as those activities that work to create and distribute fashion goods."[35] Fletcher's writing encourages us to rethink fashion durability outside the purely financial parameters of the consumer economy. That in itself is a major paradigm shift in the twenty-first century, so conditioned are we to align fashion automatically with capitalism's modes of production and consumption. As is well documented, the designer fashion system is hardwired into corporate luxury conglomerates that equate success solely with profit and link failure to the inability to accumulate wealth. The designer is, in many ways, therefore emblematic of the neoliberal subject, a figure one might deploy as a heuristic device to provide a critical understanding of fashion's interlocking logics of finance and creativity in the new era of globalized luxury.[36]

From the broader interdisciplinary perspective of Cultural Studies, mobilizing the pivotal figure of the designer, most often the public face of a label or brand, is a human way to unpick the complex intersection of art and business that structures the fashion creative economy. As in other sectors of the economy, failure, as Halberstam has noted, "goes hand in hand with capitalism."[37] Likewise, historian Scott A. Sandage talks of failure as being hard-wired into the American psyche: the dream of success is about a deep collective fear of failure, in short. "Failure is not the dark side of the American dream; it is the foundation of it."[38] These insights also recall a striking image in Stefano Massini's epic saga of American success and failure, *The Lehman Trilogy*, which begins with the arrival in the mid-nineteenth century in New York of three German Jewish immigrants, who founded the financial services firm that collapsed and filed for bankruptcy in 2008, triggering the largest global financial crisis in history.[39] Massini evokes the tightrope walker on a wire in front of Wall Street as a metaphor for risk through the analogy of falling and failing. The three Lehman brothers' first enterprise was a single dry goods store founded in 1850 in Montgomery, Alabama, called Lehman Brothers Fabrics and Clothing. Fashion and textiles have manifestly always been and remain an integral part of the intersecting histories of global finance, identity, culture, and migration.

Beyond the contemporary focus on the demise of individual designer labels, which has in fact always figured in the history of retail, it is also important to address the question of failure more systemically. In 2017, *The Business of Fashion* published a piece arguing for a radical reboot of the fashion system in light of a changing (increasingly consumer-led, post-digital) business landscape to avoid emerging designers being set up to fail. In the pre-internet commercial landscape of the late twentieth century, the path to success for a young designer was mapped out through the growth of the luxury economy: with industry buzz around a graduate collection, a designer might be scouted to become a creative director for a prestigious heritage house while having their own label underwritten by a luxury group. With the shrinking of wholesale retail and the fragmentation of the ready-to-wear market online, it now becomes increasingly difficult to operate successfully within the parameters of the "old" fashion system. On an individual level, workload pressures (with the annual rotation of seasonal concepts presented through the numerous collections) and toxic working environments, together with mental health issues, alcoholism, and substance abuse, have all been well documented as contributing to the mediatized breakdown of John Galliano in 2011 and the suicide of Alexander McQueen the previous year.[40] These questions of harm—both self and corporate—in the fashion industry also highlight how the drive to succeed precludes getting it wrong or making mistakes. A business fail is not an option. The allure of the fashion designer (shaped by the media construction and citation of an aspirational narrative of fame, glamor, and success) still lures young graduates towards a dream of status and wealth that is dependent on extrinsic recognition from opinion leaders and industry prizes.

Industry commentators have for a while now debated the breakdown of fashion: the language has changed from initial talk of "fixing" the system to documenting its full-scale collapse; as Imran Amed, editor of *The Business of Fashion* comments, the "current formulaic, corporatised, anodyne approach to fashion is not working."[41] Similarly, scholars in academic Fashion Studies have also taken a critical interest in the question of end times and the notion of collapse as central to understanding the aesthetic and cultural sensibility of the early twenty-first century.[42] In 2015 trend-forecaster Lidewij Edelkoort's *Anti_Fashion: A Manifesto for the Next Decade* proclaimed "the end of Fashion as we know it" and gave ten reasons why the system appeared obsolete—ideas that have since then entered mainstream discussions about the constraints and limitations of the consumer ecosystem.[43] Beyond retail, Edelkoort's thesis also provocatively addressed the failures of the system in terms of education, training, criticism, and design. In so doing, she was echoing the argument of journalist Teri Agins' book *The End of Fashion*, published in 1999,[44] according to which, innovation had by the turn of the century given way to profit with the structures of the industry no longer fit for purpose: the top-down pillars of criticism and promotion (fashion weeks intended principally for journalists and buyers) are, in effect, now marginalized in the contexts of the digital influencer economy, fragmented retail, and the breakdown of the traditional business model of wholesale. The idea of designing endless collections now appears increasingly anachronistic in the world of street-wear product drops and product-driven sportswear brands or those built primarily around online consumer publics.

So far, I have been arguing that to situate failure as a central pillar of fashion invites us to rethink design practices beyond the scope and parameters of luxury designer-branding, to go beyond the normative discursive and ideological framework of rise and fall, success and demise, productivity and burnout: those well-documented histories of creative fails and commercial misfires that invariably dominate the standard history of fashion. An emblematic example of this narrative tendency would be the unprofitable couture house of Christian Lacroix, which was run at a loss and later sold by the LVMH group in 2005 to the duty-free fragrance distributor, Falic Fashion Group, which continues to produce the *Eau So Couture* perfume following the bankruptcy of the house in 2009. Having relinquished the trademark of his name, Lacroix became an interior and costume designer as well as collaborating with the high-street chain Desigual on capsule collections and designer Dries Van Noten for a one-off collection (Spring/Summer 2020). This example shows that to rearticulate fashion not just as a story of success and idealization but also as a critically negative or alternative form of art and commerce also means engaging with the histories of brand failure. For example, the botched relaunch of the house of Poiret (owned by the South Korean department store franchise Shinsegae) in 2018 offers further insight into the commercial risks of reviving patrimonial couture houses. The talented Chinese-born couturière Yiqing Yin was fired after two seasons and the brand repivoted from fashion to the more profitable sectors of fragrance and cosmetics.

To get a longer view of this commercial history, let us take a sidestep from contemporary coverage of the industry to return to a seminal work in Fashion Studies, *Adorned in Dreams: Fashion and Modernity*, published in 1985, in which author Elizabeth Wilson described the aesthetics of fashion as a form of visual art originating in the early capitalist city. She was echoing the temporal and historical framework established in the early twentieth century by sociologist Georg Simmel, who had argued that fashion could be seen to occupy "the dividing-line between the past and the future, and consequently conveys a stronger feeling of the present, at least while it is at its height, than most other phenomena." Fashion, Simmel claimed, dies young and as it spreads, "it gradually goes to its doom."[45] Wilson, for her part, traced the inherent connection between the definition of a new fashion as inherently rooted in the failure of the old. Wilson argued that fashion "does not negate emotion, it simply displaces it into the realm of aesthetics." A new fashion

> starts from the rejection of the old and often an eager embracing of what was previously considered ugly; it therefore subtly undercuts its own assertion that the latest thing is somehow the final solution to the problem of how to look. But its relativism is not as senseless as at first appears; it is a statement of the unnaturalness of human

> social arrangements—which becomes very clear in the life of the city; it is a statement of the arbitrary nature of convention and even of morality; and in daring to be ugly it perhaps at the same time attempts to transcend the vulnerability of the body and its shame.[46]

Wilson illustrated this point on fashion's arbitrary daring to be ugly with reference to the designs of Jean-Paul Gaultier, quoted as locating stylistic mishaps as the essence of fashion: "People who make mistakes or dress badly are the real stylists," he commented in *Vogue* in 1984, describing his "You feel as though you've eaten too much" collection that included garments designed to look too tight as rooted in the embarrassment of failure, thereby conjoining fashion aesthetics to affective negativity.[47]

However, beyond this historical framing of failure as, in essence, the central temporal and aesthetic locus of fashion, to call for the larger structural subversion of the whole system could be considered counter-intuitive given how fashion is fundamentally hardwired into capitalism itself. Indeed, it "speaks capitalism," as Wilson pithily put it,[48] following the Marxist positioning of fashion as "the favorite child of capitalism"[49] and as "the ritual according to which the commodity fetish demands to be worshipped."[50] As fashion theorist Ulrich Lehmann has argued, with its continued focus on image and consumption, the discipline of Fashion Studies has developed predominantly as an anti-materialist discipline through a critical discourse that he contests in the following terms: "The central role of fashion as agent of capitalism manifests itself through the repositioning of the subject–object relation, the reification of mobility and sociability into predetermined consumer groups, the objectification and codification of interpersonal communication (from verbal exchange to sexuality) and the commodification of subjectivity."[51] Despite the proliferation in the early twenty-first century of diverse critical (materialist, activist, postcapitalist) movements calling into question the economic imperatives of the production of fashionable products and images, this vein of radical protest had in fact been prefigured much earlier on the runway with Gaultier's Fall/

Winter 1990 collection entitled "Stop the fashion system" which was staged as a ballet lampooning the industry, part of what sociologist Fred Davis presciently labelled as late twentieth-century anti-fashion's "vicissitudes of negation."[52] Gaultier's ironic call for systemic change has since been politically reactivated through contemporary cultural concerns with the long-term sustainability of globalized production and consumption and a corrective slowing down of the industry, as well as contestation of the industry's highly problematic politics of race and practices of cultural appropriation.[53] Clearly, any critical understanding of failure in fashion today should also be extended to include the numerous branded instances of cultural insensitivity or blatant racism such as Dolce and Gabbana's offensive "Eating with Chopsticks" campaign video in 2018 that was called out by Instagram watchdog group, Diet Prada, leading to calls for a boycott of the brand in China.

In sum, the many structural failings of the fashion system indicate the urgent need for a paradigm shift that would respond not only to the macro-industrial questions of sustainability, inequality, and exploitation, but also take account of the technological questions of craft and digital innovation, and factor in the broader cultural questions of identity, inclusivity, and diversity. This alternative history of fashion therefore needs to include those designers whose career trajectories and posthumous appraisal were limited by oppressive cultural and political hierarchies of gender and race.[54] This shift is partly generational and the cultural values of younger generations of emerging designers, influenced so much by the codes and styles of digital media, are also impacting on the new trends that draw on an aesthetics of failure, to which we now turn our attention.

2 AESTHETICS OF FAILURE

What is a fashion fail? Why does failure matter to how we dress? As well as envisioning failure structurally as an important part of the fashion system, a common-sense approach to the topic would also ask the straightforward question of how ordinary people feel about dressing badly or failing to get it right. Vox populi might well attribute poor dress to personal taste, psychological issues such as a lack of self-confidence or else technical issues such as poor fit or contextual ones such as misjudging the occasion. Dress failure might also include a lack of knowledge, lack of interest, restrictive dress norms or customs, body image and accessibility issues as well as time constraints and financial considerations. In an age marked by the hyper-consumption of fashionable clothing, people are nonetheless still as anxious about dress or fear failing to get fashion right according to different social situations, both formal and informal.

In reality, fast fashion does not help people to dress "well" or "better" or avoid making mistakes; it just endlessly multiplies consumer options, making the threat of failure ever-present. However, one might also wonder whether the whole outdated notion of failing to dress well, dependent as it is on class-based, prescriptive norms of "good" and "bad" taste, still even resonates in a post-Internet age marked by the integration of online sensibilities like *fugly*, *wierdcore*, and other DIY-style meme-based aesthetics into the broader popular culture. Nonetheless, despite the chaotic proliferation of competing fashion trends, styles, concepts, and aesthetics, recalcitrant feelings of anxiety and embarrassment remain around dress despite (or perhaps due to) widespread access to fashion and beauty tutorials online and make-over reality shows on TV that all essentially try to expose and contain failure.[1]

The Negative Art of Dress

Sophie Woodward's ethnographic research into why women wear what they wear underscores the "internal ambivalence" in the moment of dressing.[2] The key questions involved in the everyday aesthetics of dress (Does this go? Is this me?), Woodward argues, structure the personal narratives of identity as they intersect with the commercial preoccupations of consumer fashion. Drawing on anthropologist Daniel Miller's adoption of the Hegelian concept of objectification, Woodward examines getting dressed "as a process of self-construction which involves seeing the self in an external material form."[3] She observes that part of this process of objectification invariably involves the risk of failure, "that the person cannot live up to the items of clothing or that the item will betray the wearer."[4] Measuring self-image and the harsh reality of the mirror image against the idealized projections and commercial fantasies of the fashion industry means the "potential for failure is immense; when coupled with the burdens on successfully expressing one's self, there is little wonder the act of dressing becomes such an anxious act."[5] Alison Clarke and Daniel Miller have further examined how anxiety determines what people wear. Their article aims to move away from the tendency in Fashion Studies to privilege research into the commercial imperatives of the fashion industry rather than an experience of fashion and dress as an everyday practice governed by social conventions and pressures that are expressed "primarily as a form of anxiety over potential social embarrassment."[6]

This socio-anthropological framing of the everyday experience of dress in relation to the norms and idealizations of the fashion industry also leads us back to the classic theoretical literature of fashion in modernity that includes mention of failure—both systemic and individual. Sociologist Anthony Giddens defines modernity precisely as the "interconnection between the two 'extremes' of extensionality and intentionality: globalising influences on the one hand and personal disposition on the other."[7] Adapting this inherent tension to the arena of fashion, Christopher Breward and Caroline Evans have described it as a tool to interrogate "the subjective experience of modern life," as both "a market-driven cycle of consumer desire and demand" and "a modern mechanism for the fabrication of the self."[8]

Ulrich Lehmann's book *Tigersprung: Fashion in Modernity* provides a full account of the philosophical idea of modernity in fashion following theorists and writers after Marx who have situated the "hallmark of modernity" in "the ever-growing objectification of society."[9] Through its layers of historical quotation, "fashion fuses the thesis (the eternal or classical ideal) with its antithesis (the openly contemporary)."[10] To draw out the inbuilt contradictions in the idea of fashion, Lehmann points us in the direction of Simmel and Benjamin, two important theorists of fashion, whose writings still resonate for us in the context of failure. Famous for his thesis on the subject according to which fashion articulates the contradiction between two antagonistic principles: imitation (uniformity or integration according to the dictates of style) versus differentiation (the personal conception of style or expression of individuality), Simmel also noted that even those who pay no heed to fashion nonetheless accept its forms by embodying it through negation rather than through exaggeration.[11] This question of negation is therefore crucial to theorizing failure in fashion; as is the question of time.

Benjamin, for his part, posited temporality (the *time* of history) as fashion's distinctive mechanism. His aesthetic was conjured up from the commodity form, the epitome of which paradoxically is "the cult of fashion, in which the familiar returns with some slight variation, the very old and the very new caught up together in some oxymoronic logic of identity-in-difference."[12] Benjamin's epistemology of fashion consisted of dialectical images containing fragments and quotations from the past as constituting its dynamic. In his 1940 *Theses on the Philosophy of History* he wrote:

> Fashion has a flair for the topical, no matter where it stirs in the thickets of long ago; it is a tiger's leap into the past. This jump, however, takes place in an arena where the ruling class gives the commands. The same leap in the open air of history is the dialectical one, which is how Marx understood the revolution.[13]

As Philipp Ekardt has argued, Benjamin departed from Simmel's analysis of fashion's ontological modes to posit fashion as "a measure of time."[14] The discontinuous nature of fashion time and fashion's disjunctive interpretation of history relate to the formal dialectic of style: the abrupt transition from what is in or out of fashion, the cycles and rhythms that denote what is desirable and what is discarded at any given moment. The "overly common" and the "particularly old" converge to shape what is out of fashion. To quote at length from Ekardt's reading of the outdated:

> Such a relegation of a given style, taste, look, etc. to the realm of the *démodé* (i.e. the generation of the outmoded) is as much a product of fashion as is the resuscitation of the obsolete (under the right conditions). Fashion not only produces *both*, in and out; both are also two sides of a similar operation, namely the qualification of a temporal relationship with aesthetic and formal manifestations (about to be) situated in the past.[15]

Ekardt therefore distinguishes between Simmel's straightforward view of the past as providing the raw materials for the emergence of new fashions in the present and Benjamin's more complex view of fashion as structured more like a palimpsest, a layering of the past that is constantly rearticulated through the process of design.[16] Accordingly, the whole point of fashion—its ideology, so to speak—derives from its temporal investment in newness and the inevitability of failure, "its endless reiteration of novelty and obsolescence, each caught in an endlessly self-canceling relationship with the other."[17]

In *The Arcades Project*, an unfinished collection of documentation on urban life, art, and culture amassed between 1927 and the author's death in 1940, Benjamin also underlined fashion's temporal logic as trading in and switching between the extremes of frivolity and death,[18] which echoed both Simmel's point on how fashions invariably die young and philosopher Giacomo Leopardi's dialogue between fashion and death in his 1824 poem, a line from which Benjamin reproduced as an epigraph at the start of his constellation of thoughts and quotations on fashion.

Conversely, the other epigraph ("Nothing dies; all is transformed") is a quotation from the work of the French nineteenth-century novelist Honoré de Balzac.[19] As we move towards a discussion of the popular aesthetic forms taken by failure in contemporary fashion, let us first turn to Balzac as a model for his pointed vision of the importance of dress and surface to the workings of capitalist modernity. He was singled out by Marxist literary historian Georg Lukács as illustrating the capitalization of the bourgeois spirit in how his venal tales of devouring ambition and material greed deployed fashionable clothing, interior décor, and personal accessories as key indicators of social success and the shameful risks of failure.[20]

Critic Franco Moretti's sociological reading of Balzac, in which the materialistic dynamics of ambition, appearance, and self-invention are measured by the surface forms they take more than by their actual content, shows how his work has an obvious application to historical and theoretical articulations of fashion. More than the accumulation of wealth and social status, more than money and power, fashion is in Balzac's novel *Lost Illusions* (1837–43) the arbitrary key to success, however fleeting. Lucien Chardon, the parvenu protagonist, an ambitious poet from the provinces, who adopts his mother's noble surname de Rubempré upon arrival in Paris, is described by Moretti as incarnating the mercantile spirit of the times, figured as "a fashionable commodity: discovered, put on the market, triumphant, out of style, thrown away."[21] Indeed, Lucien's submission to the superficial charms of Parisian life equates to a negation of self and individuality, in this reading, an admonition of the traps of urban modernity. Success, then, in the nineteenth-century sense that still, at least in part, holds sway for us nearly two centuries later, is essentially about how individuals mediate the materialist ecosystem of the capitalist metropolis. (Needless to say, twenty-first century success—in fashion as in other creative sectors—is clearly as much conditioned and driven by the interlocking economic mechanisms of global and digital interconnectivity as by the specific cultural dynamics of the international urban centers of design and creativity.)

In Balzac's tale, Lucien's natural beauty is an asset to be exploited in his transformation from penniless provincial poet to unprincipled urbane journalist. Upon arrival in Paris, he is shamefully aware of his own sartorial failings; the vulgarity and ugliness of his attire is all the more shocking alongside the smartly dressed peacocks adorning the Parisian public stage.[22] Balzac's narrator describes Lucien's sense of belittlement having been a somebody at home only to become a nobody in Paris. He describes how "those who pass too abruptly from the one to the other experience a feeling of annihilation,"[23] a rather extreme state of mind simply for dressing poorly. Lucien is mistaken for a domestic by footmen and the narrator is at pains to emphasize prophetically the importance of costume "for those who wish to appear to have what they do not have, because that is often the best way of getting it later on."[24] Deploring his image for betraying his origins as an apothecary's son, a lowly member of the professional classes, Lucien admires the public *mise en scène* of dandified masculinity on display on the Faubourg Saint-Germain. His attraction to Madame de Bargeton, with whom he has eloped, wanes as soon as they are exposed to the harsh glare of Parisian social mores. To dispel his feelings of shame and adapt to the elevated company of the Marquise d'Espard, in whose theatre box Lucien and his mistress are invited to spend an evening in society, he spends all his savings on a brash green frockcoat, which is ridiculed by the attendant beau monde, an elite stratum both admired and despised in Balzac's ambivalent narration of events. Indeed, Lucien might be derided as a prototypical country cousin by polite society but the novel traces his revenge, an ambitious rise and fall through the business of cultural journalism. The overall ambivalence about fashion as an index of success and failure is conveyed through an excessive semiotic attention to decorative and sartorial detail, which even includes the promotional name-checking of Parisian tailors.[25] In director Xavier Giannoli's 2021 film adaptation, the theatre scene is altered to focus our attention on Lucien's ludicrous hair-style more than his attire, a demonstration of ornamental excess that is read as a transparent sign of the character's innate vulgarity according to the materialistic codes and snobbish values of Balzac's world.

Cast in the role of Nathan d'Anastazio, the idealistic novelist who is Lucien's frenemy, the Quebecois actor and director, Xavier Dolan, brought out the film's queer subtext. His ambivalent perspective frames the narrative through an intrusive voice-over and a queer gaze—the lingering voyeuristic shots of actor Benjamin Voisin's naked body are intended to underline Lucien's later objectified status as a kept boy. In parallel, queer critic Madison Moore deploys Balzac's 1835 novel *Old Goriot* as an illustration of class shaming and sartorial failure when the young parvenu Eugène de Rastignac arrives at a costume ball splattered with mud, thereby indicating his lowly social status.[26]

As we now consider more fully the commercial aesthetics of failure in contemporary fashion, let us also keep in mind the queer lens through which much popular media and culture is articulated and reprocessed, particularly the "negative" or "failed" design sensibilities of kitsch, camp, ugly, and vulgar. Dolan, who has also modelled for Louis Vuitton menswear, is a filmmaker whose stylized cinema is heavily invested in fashion and décor. Working as costume designer on all his own films, Dolan's approach to narrative through styling shows how he places the look of popular fashion at the heart of his stories by making ironic use of multiple surfaces to punctuate the dramatic tension and shape the worlds that he is imagining. His cinema of excess ambitiously deploys camp hyperbole and proliferating surfaces as the formal means to embed individual stories of love, longing, and desire within cultural questions of conflict, constraint, and power. The intentionally failed taste and vulgar fashions of his lower middle-class suburban mothers raise questions of age, femininity, and class in relation to the handling of costume design. This creative cultivation of lowbrow styling, one that is intentionally tasteless, might be a case of "naïve camp" in cultural critic Susan Sontag's understanding of a form of "seriousness that fails,"[27] but it also finds more high-brow parallels in designer fashion, particularly in the contemporaneous trend for re-aestheticized ugly styles and in the "new baroque" sensibility noted in fashion history. Rather than simply denoting outlandish garments, the "new baroque" designs are based on the assumption that "a desire for excess is the norm. They improvise with the leftovers of other styles: they are testing new ground, without the compromise of established taste."[28] The desire for excess is indeed the norm in fashion's post-digital aesthetics of failure.

Fashion and Failure After Digital

Fugly is the new pretty—at least according to the rhetoric of popular fashion media. Failed aesthetics were reported to be dominating fashion by the early 2020s with the rise of so-called "ugly beauty," which one might view, in part, as a rejection of the "clean girl" beauty trend of the 2010s represented by white social media influencers and celebrities. It could also be seen as a rejection of the bland corporate type of luxury style associated with high-end U.S. labels like Michael Kors, Narciso Rodriguez, or Tory Burch, which formed part of "the return of 'pretty'" in minimalist fashion through the 2000s.[29] The rise of ugliness in fashion is also symptomatic of the continued cross-fertilization between the catwalk and the sidewalk, and between designer-branded fashion and digital screen styles, particularly Instagrammable and meme-friendly looks that have broad cross-over appeal. Fashion media also reported the return of pencil-thin eyebrows and unblended foundation, capri pants, crop tops and fringed cowboy boots, and the ubiquity of the once functional but now highly desirable crocs. This selection forms part of the chaotic dissemination of referential online styles that are channeled through social media platforms like TikTok and vulgarized through the mass media narratives of TV. Take as an example of this cross-platform mechanism Jonathan Anderson's 3-D designed pigeon clutch, which went viral as part of the online "weirdcore" aesthetic after it adorned actress Sarah Jessica Parker in the second series of the *Sex and the City* spin-off show, *And Just Like That*, in 2023.

Alternative styles dominate platforms like TikTok, which has paved the way for a digital aesthetic in which so-called Gen Z fashions are recycled from nostalgic projections of the styles of the 1990s and early 2000s. The proliferation of "core" or "girl" aesthetics (cottagecore, weirdcore, VSCO girl, witchtok, and so forth) are, in essence, appearance-based trends without any ideological content or formal coherence. Weirdgirl, for example, showcases kitsch accessories in a maximal way, mixing and matching clashing patterns and textures,

FIGURE 5 Weirdcore: Designer Jonathan Anderson's 3D printed pigeon clutch, here displayed in the Memorabile, Ipermoda exhibition, MAXXI museum Rome, 2024–5.

and capitalizing on a nostalgia for pop culture of the 1990s. The launch in 2020 of the Marc Jacobs line Heaven, co-designed by Ava Nirui, which is popular with celebrity models like Kendall Jenner, aimed specifically to target Gen Z consumers with Y-2-K-inspired collections and collabs that drop monthly, thereby contributing to over-production and conforming to the economic logic of the feed in which brands pump out digital content relentlessly.

To get a longer, more historically informed view of this digital fashion trend that elevates the kitsch object, it is worthwhile returning to earlier theoretical perspectives, notably to Simmel's seminal essay in which the author argued that through its cycles of arbitrary aesthetic prescription, sometimes promoting as in vogue a series of "ugly and repugnant things," fashion seems "desirous of exhibiting its power by getting us to adopt the most atrocious things for its sake alone."[30] In a similar vein, in his *Economics of Fashion*, published in 1928, Paul H. Nystrom contended that fashion, not to be flouted or rejected at any cost, exerted considerable power over ordinary consumers' social behavior:

> The influence of fashion over the human mind is such as to make a style, when accepted, seem beautiful, no matter how hideous it may appear at other times when not in fashion. It is hard to believe that the hoop skirt, the bustle and the leg o'mutton sleeve were once considered very charming and highly appropriate. No doubt the present fashions will in time seem just as ridiculous and even, possibly, as hideous as do these past styles seem to us now.[31]

Wearing out-of-fashion items will inevitably illicit "quizzical looks, doubtful stares, and critical estimates."[32] The aesthetic judgment of others is clearly central to failure. The fear of being seen to be "queer" (sic) or just plain odd, conceived as a state of failed identity, is enough to ensure obedience to the codifications of fashion. In a later section of *Economics of Fashion*, Nystrom further detailed how the so-called Parisian dictators of style had on occasion failed to predict consumer tastes or had tried to bring back articles of apparel that were going out of fashion such as ostrich feathers. Predictions such as wider hats and tailored suits were often repeated failures in women's wear through the 1920s.

Popular fashion's ongoing elevation of the oxymoronic concept of "ugly beauty" through the mash-up of sartorial signifiers predates the digital culture of the early twenty-first century. Journalist Robin Givhan reported on the self-consciously ugly trends appearing on the runway through the 1990s, which included clothes that looked intentionally cheap, poor, and unattractive so as to emphasize utility and practicality of the everyday or the ordinary.[33] Miuccia Prada, in particular, made intentionally ugly garments legitimate on the catwalks of Milan through her charming bad taste aesthetic. "If I have done anything," she commented, "it is to make ugly appealing. In fact, most of my work is concerned with destroying—or at least deconstructing—conventional ideas of beauty, of the generic appeal of the beautiful, glamorous, bourgeois woman. [...] The investigation of ugliness is, to me, more interesting than the bourgeois idea of beauty."[34] Indeed, it was the Prada Spring/Summer 1996 collection, entitled "Banal Eccentricity" that first referenced the vintage pretty/ugly hues of chocolate brown of the 1970s, drawing on extremely unfashionable palettes, silhouettes, and materials and, paradoxically, making them fashionable again. Prada's skill, in short, lies in reassembling conventionally ugly concepts as part of a coherent aesthetic proposition. Moreover, ugliness in fashion is also therefore as much a temporal as an anti-aesthetic concept. To provide a theoretical parallel to Prada's postmodern aesthetic sensibility, philosopher Giorgio Agamben has deployed fashion precisely to illustrate his thesis of contemporariness as "a singular relationship with one's own time, which adheres to it and, at the same time, keeps a distance from it."[35] Positing disjunction and anachronism, distancing and proximity, as the overarching mechanisms that structure our relationship to contemporariness and time, he employs fashion's discontinuous temporality (of being in and then out of fashion; of being desirable one moment and unattractive the next) to indicate a dynamic tension between a "not yet" and a "no more."[36]

In the commercial arena of fashion, there is also clearly a convergence of two strands of ugly: a post-ironic articulation through digital pop culture alongside the more ostensibly artful conception of high fashion designers like Rei Kawakubo (for Comme des Garçons), for example, whose designs also dialogue with the aesthetic strangeness of the avant-garde.[37] As cultural theorist Mark Cousins argued in his series of essays on the subject, the ugly has always been relegated to negation, as that which cannot be considered aesthetic (in the sense of the beautiful), but it also exceeds that definition. Ugliness has "a real and independent dimension in which it is experienced as that which is there and which should not be there."[38] Detaching the ugly from the beautiful, giving it an artistic autonomy would also imply (through the processes of hyper-commodification of late capitalist consumer culture) an articulation with other "failed" aesthetic categories traditionally relegated to the "unartful," such as the vulgar, the kitsch, and the camp.[39] These categories, traditionally considered tacky or trashy, trivial or queer, banished from aesthetic appraisal as forms of "failed" art, are, in fact, key intersecting strands in commercial culture's repertoire of sensibilities and styles.

Categories of Failure: Vulgar, Kitsch, Camp

For the purposes of our discussion of failed aesthetics, let's take a twofold definition of the vulgar, meant to signify that which is either distasteful (in the sense of rude, indecent, offensive, coarse, crude, racy, risqué, naughty, or obscene); or else tasteless (in the sense of unrefined, tawdry, ostentatious, kitsch, brassy, garish, flashy, flamboyant, or unfashionable). The inverse therefore would denote a style that is tasteful, inoffensive, clean, moral, pure, aesthetic, decent, refined, artistic, beautiful, and fashionable. Historically, the dominant ways of discerning sartorial fashion rely on the traditional idealist focus of aesthetics, whereby the general understandings of elegance and luxury are indexed to the value of objects of beauty. In order to fully engage with the eclectic chaotic styles of popular post-digital fashion, both designer-branded and street/screen styles, we therefore need to examine the inverse of the artistically refined, tasteful or elegant styles, that which gives them meaning and value—the ugly, the distasteful, and the vulgar.

To vulgarize is both to make popular and to degrade and debase. In the introduction to a literary history of vulgarity and modernity, historian Bertrand Buffon laments contemporary mass-media manifestations of the omnipresent phenomenon as illustrative of an "intemperate modernity," attributing the origins of the term "vulgarity" to writer Madame de Staël, whose neologism from 1802 was intended to describe a distinct lack of elegance in both manner and style.[40] Buffon then proceeds to take Balzac's fictions of nineteenth-century materialism mentioned previously as emblematic of the growth through the century of a society obsessed with ostentation, shaping an understanding of good taste and sophisticated manners through the display of material objects, through consumer fetishism—viewed through the critical lens of Marxist thought as "part of a historically particular regime of circulation of consumer goods to which advertising, design and display—a whole apparatus of 'commodity aesthetics'—is central."[41]

As we saw with the case of Balzac's *Lost Illusions*, commodity aesthetics have formed a central part of the fabric of urban life in the literary and artistic representations of the world's metropolitan centers of power and influence of the last two centuries and have in large part generated the cultural mythology of the fashion capitals of Paris, London, and New York. If we situate the common use of the term vulgar, therefore, as a powerful and repressive marker of class privilege, then the opening to Edith Wharton's 1920 novel *The Age of Innocence*, her retrospective tale of late nineteenth-century high-society manners, offers an exemplary illustration of the historical role of dress in defining and policing good taste. It also combines both strands of the vulgar—the crude and the offensive. The novel opens at a New York opera house. As the sophisticated Newland Archer scrutinizes his fiancée, May Welland's box, he is disturbed by the unexpected arrival of her cousin, the glamorous but scandalous countess Ellen Olenska, the dissolution of whose marriage has exposed her to the judgment—both envious and lustful—of the New York beau monde. It is precisely Olenska's style of dress that shocks society: "The suggestion of this headdress, which gave her what was then called a 'Josephine look,' was carried out in the cut of the dark blue velvet gown rather theatrically caught up under her bosom by a girdle with a large old-fashioned clasp." The countess proceeds to focus her attention on the stage "revealing, as she leaned forward, a little more shoulder and bosom than New York was accustomed to seeing, at least in ladies who had reasons for wishing to pass unnoticed."[42] Vulgar dress is therefore revealed as the prime indicator of the character's public shame, at least in the codified class structure of Wharton's world of surface hypocrisy. Archer is quick to judge his betrothed's racy cousin, seemingly so careless of the dictates of Taste: Wharton capitalizes the concept to emphasize its stranglehold on attitudes and behavior. "Few things," she writes, "seemed to Newland Archer more awful than an offence against 'Taste,' that far-off divinity of whom 'Form' was the mere visible representative and vicegerent."[43] In Martin Scorsese's lavish 1993 film adaptation, the vulgar is conveyed by revealing the countess's skin and also by the choice of actress playing her: the popular Hollywood star Michelle Pfeiffer, whose naturalistic acting style complemented the scandalous modernity of the character through comportment and movements that jar with the period setting of the late nineteenth century.

This manifest policing of taste, as Pierre Bourdieu later revealed in his sociology of distinction, is essentially rooted in a contempt for "lower" class or popular cultural expressions and pleasures. He argued that the Enlightenment philosopher Immanuel Kant's dominant aesthetic principle of pure taste was "nothing other than a refusal, a disgust—a disgust for objects which impose enjoyment and a disgust for the crude, vulgar taste which revels in this imposed enjoyment."[44] So-called failed taste is therefore, according to Bourdieu, determined by the symbolic displacements of a bourgeois culture that articulates economic power as the power to distance basic necessity. Kant's dominant aesthetic principle of pure taste was, according to Bourdieu, a refusal or a disgust of pleasure, or rather a disgust of the vulgarity of enjoyment. This point clearly echoes the thesis earlier formulated at the turn of the twentieth century by economist Thorstein Veblen, who had dissected the class-codification of Western definitions of taste and beauty as part of the "code of reputability in matters of dress," any departures from which are deemed "offensive to our taste, supposedly as being departures from aesthetic truth."[45] Dismissing the idea of intrinsic beauty in matters of sartorial fashion, Veblen emphasized the very arbitrary nature of what is deemed fashionable in any one season. Success in beauty is therefore indexed to reputability—the vulgar marked out as that which is to be discarded.

However, more often than not, what is discarded from an idealist history of fashion is often not just the aesthetically displeasing but rather the clothing of ordinary people—the vulgar simply referring to pieces of everyday clothing. Indeed, rather than position the vulgar as pervasive within contemporary culture, it should perhaps be seen as the exception to the rule of uniformity and normalcy that governs the social adoption of fashionable clothing. As Cheryl Buckley and Hazel Clark have argued, "scholarship in fashion has tended to focus on the avant-garde, the extraordinary and the unusual. Indeed, within fashion's discourses, the truly 'ordinary' remains elusive."[46] The theoretical focus on fashion's transience as the central tenet of urban modernity (in particular through the impact of the writings of poet, essayist, and art critic Charles Baudelaire on the ontology of fashion) has led to an epistemological preference for the spectacular as opposed to the everyday practices of dress as lived or embodied experience, part of a decentered definition of fashion as, in essence, an art of the vulgar and a *popular* art form par excellence. The vulgar therefore is not simply a class-based category of failed taste; rather, through its multiple strategies of copying and appropriation it refers equally to fashion's anti-linear scrambling of time. The vulgar, like other negative or failed aesthetic categories, is therefore also a temporal marker of history.

Showing off, breaking the rules, flouting convention: the vulgar, as psychoanalytic writer Adam Phillips remarks, is manifestly about "the wrong people enjoying the wrong pleasures."[47] In her review of the *The Vulgar: Fashion Redefined* exhibition in London in 2016, which sought to reassess the creativity of the vulgar in fashion history, Elizabeth Wilson locates its emancipatory potential in its challenge to "authoritarian modes of being."[48] The fashion industry has tended historically to reproduce a standard monolithic notion of good (and bad) taste, of idealized bodies and acceptable sexualities, the glaring contradiction being that fashion itself is commonly held to be vulgar precisely because of its commercial nature and industrial structure.[49] The vulgar, as Wilson goes on to explain, is also clearly centered around the postmodern copying, quoting, and recycling of new ideas and retrieved concepts. The accelerated cycles of consumer fashion define the tenor of the popular through fashion's obsessive reprocessing of formerly "low-brow" aesthetic references.

In contemporary fashion, the most obvious instance of the combination of post-ironic versions of vulgar and ugly is designer Demna Gvasalia's re-appropriation, transformation, and elevation of the ordinary and everyday into a fashionable object of desire (the Uber Eats bag, the DHL delivery t-shirt, bulky track sneakers, oversize ill-fitting jeans, neon croc shoes with cartoon badges) for Vetements and Balenciaga—symptomatic of the commercial importance of meme-based branded products. This larger trend for digital elevation has also seen the launch of Lidl sneakers and the rejuvenation of Birkenstocks, a brand that has discarded its unfashionable reputation for orthopedic comfort and functionality by collaborating with designer labels such as Jil Sander and Rick Owens. Indeed, this whole sensibility deriving from online meme culture shows how the impact of digital on popular fashion

FIGURE 6 Designer Demna Gvasalia attends the 2021 CFDA Fashion Awards in New York City.

involves what scholar Nick Douglas has called "internet ugly" to denote a self-consciously ironic and self-deprecating style that valorizes imperfections by elevating the sloppy and the amateurish through aesthetic failure.[50] Balenciaga's resurrection of formerly devalued items of dress is a commercial maneuver that is in fact an integral part of the brand's history (or DNA, in marketing terms): the founder, Cristóbal Balenciaga did something similar by elevating the *vareuse* tunics in 1951. This design territory has been vocally defended by the brand's designer and was in the late 2010s and early 2020s prized as the ultimate statement of un-fashion. It was also illustrative of the fashion industry's wider embrace of entertainment culture—Demna's integration of a specially commissioned episode of *The Simpsons* for the Balenciaga Spring/Summer 2022 collection or the catwalk presentation in Hollywood for the pre-fall 2024 collection are further examples of the brand's trans-media entertainment strategy. In an age in which curating replaces creativity, figures like Demna (branded familiarly by his first name) can thus be interpreted through the lens of post-digital fashion: particularly the semiotic play with memes and the connective logic of copying, citation, and influence, which has led the designer to the contradictory position of both castigating and feeding fashion as an all-devouring form of media spectacle.

The vulgar, however, is not just concerned with the spectacle of popular entertainment; in its more extreme manifestations, it can also be deployed to shock and cause offense. Take, for instance, Rick Owens' Fall/Winter 2015 collection, which was notorious for exposing the genitalia of his male models and which was seen as a challenge to the patriarchal symbolic power of the phallus by revealing its diminished physical reality. This vein of camp humor, also present in Jeremy Scott's flamboyantly pop-inspired aesthetic for the Italian label Moschino, is central to the valorization of bad taste, and inherent to the vulgar, the ugly, and the camp as conjoining negative or failed aesthetic sensibilities. Patricia A. Morton locates the ugliness of camp "in its excessiveness, its lack of wholeness, its valorization of bad taste, its deployment of incongruity and its recuperation of past images, objects and products that have lost their value."[51] The ugly object is therefore transformed into a camp one through the pleasure taken in the awful. Scott's gaudy pop collections for the storied Italian brand tended to rework iconic American commercial iconography (the bright yellow McDonald's logo printed on red dresses) following the visual heritage of mid-century pop art's investment in consumerism and demonstrating how the vulgar is itself inherently inscribed within the vast array of visual language, signage, and iconicity of popular media-culture (particularly film, pop art, and advertising). The valorization of bad taste in pop art's DNA also shows how the ugly has always been historically associated with forms of creative imperfection and failure.

In his aesthetic history of ugliness, Umberto Eco followed Bourdieu's lead in drawing on the social hierarchy of taste involved in diminishing the tastes of the "lower" classes as ridiculous and discriminating against the upwardly mobile nouveau riche "who, in order to show off his wealth, exceeds the limits assigned by the dominant aesthetic sensibility to 'good taste'."[52] It is precisely the social policing of taste that determines the exclusion of camp, ugly, vulgar, and other "failed" tastes as marginal and queer. "Camp," Eco comments in relation to the influential notes penned by Sontag on the subject,

> is not measured by the beauty of something but on the extent of its artifice and stylization, and it is not defined so much as a style but as the capacity to consider the style of others. To be camp, objects must possess some exaggeration or marginal aspect ..., as well as a certain degree of vulgarity, even when there is a claim to refinement.[53]

The vulgar is therefore inherently context-dependent; its aesthetic parameters depend on the appraisal of an audience and on the judgment of others. Vulgar, like camp and other failed sensibilities, is invariably in the eye of the beholder.

The creative logic of camp, Sontag famously argued, lies precisely in its aesthetic sensibility of "failed seriousness," in its ironic transvaluation of vulgar objects, tastes, and styles. The lover of camp takes delight in the vulgar to subvert serious (straight, bourgeois, orthodox) categories of taste. With its heady mix of the ostentatious, the excessive, the indecent, and the obscene, camp might, in short, be defined as vulgar with a queer sense of humor. Sontag's original hypothesis held camp to work precisely through its failure to get it quite right. So, to discuss the aesthetic of a designer like Jeremy Scott, for example, is inevitably to be confronted by the question of how to judge a design that is purposefully "off": an aesthetic vision that is so awful, it's good, to paraphrase Sontag.

Returning to the negative aesthetic theories of Adorno, critics Adam Geczy and Vicki Karaminas agree that the categories under consideration here are indeed tenuous ones: "Because kitsch is synonymous with the culture industry, it tends to eclipse the notion of the ugly, although they are closely related."[54] The nebulousness of a term like kitsch as a form of "failed" fashion is such that it becomes "an ersatz term for everything that happens to be undesirable (and unfashionable) at any particular time."[55] Geczy and Karaminas proceed to examine instances of camp and kitsch in fashion that seek to destabilize standard notions of "good taste" in tandem with the queer challenge to fixed gender and sexual identities. Indeed, one might add that the new age of kitsch in the commodified aesthetics of fashion, design, and consumer culture—a neo-kitsch sensibility—involves the conjugation of two paradoxical strands of media-culture: a post-ironic sensibility of performance on social media platforms like TikTok blended with a post-conformist presentation of self, achieved by projecting a curated version of one's individualism through self-consciously ugly and chaotically styled looks. This aesthetic—that marketers tend to associate demographically with post-millennial Gen Z and was reported to dominate popular fashion by the mid-2020s—is associated with the rejection of pre-processed, late-stage capitalist fashion (both luxury and fast fashion) in favor of the resurrection of scuzzy Y-2-K styles inspired by the studiously unpolished, "failed" looks of pop stars like Charlie XCX or it-girls

FIGURE 7 Designer Francisco Terra walks the runway during the Neith Nyer Spring/Summer 2018 show, Paris.

like Julia Fox. Failure in the world of post-digital styling is all in the reference; ugliness is in the eye of the beholder. Needless to add that these unflattering looks sampled from a range of lowbrow sources are associated with conventionally attractive, young, slim bodies, indicating an elitist blind spot in fashion's rhetoric of inclusivity. Moreover, many of social media's "concepts" of girlhood—consumer articulations of femininity that are gimmicks more than aesthetics—also routinely form part of a conservative plundering of the queer performance styles of trans women of color: take as an example the mainstream recuperation in 2024 of content creator Jools Lebron's droll catchphrase—"very demure, very mindful, very cutesy"—ironically advocating a proper, aspirational type of feminine self-presentation, which was immediately taken up by stars and celebrities, telecommunications brands (Verizon), and entertainment platforms (Netflix) alike to become a digital PR micro-moment.

One last example with which to close our discussion of fashion's failed aesthetics: the independent Brazilian designer Francisco Terra, who flies below the radar, has nonetheless shown his collections at Paris fashion week and was a finalist for the ANDAM prize in 2018. His designs have embraced a democratic vision of bad taste for all as the distinctive visual code of his emerging label, Neith Nyer. Thrift shopping and pre-owned clothes are his main sources of inspiration; re-use underpins his design process. His Spring/Summer 2018 collection elevated excess through an eclectic array of cheap-looking garments and accessories including fringed cowboy boots, crystals on vintage T-shirts, fake furs, and shiny silver boddices—redolent of the kitsch of shiny things and the vulgar connotations of reflective surfaces. For Fall/Winter 2018/2019, Terra sought to blur the lines between vulgarity and elegance, a key strategy in both the aesthetics of failure and contemporary fashion's more generalized boundary blurring after postmodernity. Neith Nyer is a prime example of a contemporary designer brand that eschews the pretentions of high art to engage with the popular ways of challenging the ideals of fashion. This includes the two stands of the vulgar, combining the unrefined

FIGURE 8 Neith Nyer runway, Paris fashion week, menswear Spring/Summer 2022.

and the distasteful: homemade-looking DIY techniques (like taking in the seams of the clothes and topstitching them to refit the garment), cone-shaped bras slit in the middle to show the nipple and long, skin-revealing velvet dresses. The press release for the show explained the rationale as an attempt to answer a seemingly straightforward but recurring question that continues to stimulate and provoke debate in fashion and the visual arts: what precisely *is* bad taste?

3
FAME AND FAILURE

Fame is notoriously fickle. It is also about failure, a fact reinforced by the language of rising and falling stars or the imagery of meteoric rise and sunken dreams. Celebrity status, one might add, is not only one of the most obvious manifestations of success in our performance-based, media-driven society but also an underlying source of harm. The negative narratives of failure are central to the value and circulation of fame within our public discourse. One way or another, success tends to get measured as renown.

In his survey of the importance of stars to a critical appreciation of film, Richard Dyer described how the dominant image of stardom had emerged as a version of the myth of the American Dream, shaped by discourses of "consumption, success and ordinariness."[1] Failure is also articulated as a Hollywood counter-narrative said to sour the dream. Adapting Dyer's insights to the arena of popular celebrity culture, Sean Redmond emphasizes the element of suffering in fame, its collapse and dissolution—hence the recurrent media reports of celebrities falling apart or coming undone through mental illness, suffering, and addiction. Reference is also made to historian Leo Braudy's description of the disintegration of the self through fame, the celebrity ending up a damaged self "used and discarded by the mechanistic excesses of capitalism."[2] Braudy detailed how "the performer who hits the top only to disintegrate into a psychic mess has been around in various guises since the middle of the nineteenth century."[3]

Like Hollywood, fashion too is a destroyer, at least according to popular myth. One strand of this negative discourse involves a combination of scandal and excess, both of which have been associated with the figure of the fashion designer since the birth of haute couture in the mid-nineteenth century up until the present-day digital performance of authenticity and personality on social media platforms. Representations of designers often trade in romanticized images of creative artists; today's designers, however, are more often promoted by the industry as creative directors, as communicators who tailor creativity to the commercial imperatives of brands; more than artisans, they are increasingly cross-platform managers under sustained commercial pressure to succeed at all times.

In *The Penguin Book of Twentieth-Century Fashion Writing*, editor Judith Watt explains that "the story of twentieth-century fashion is the story of the designer: the establishment of the couturier at its start and the power of haute couture and the designer label at its end."[4] Watt's schematic overview is bookended by the impact on Paris fashion of two notable Englishmen: the originator of haute couture, Charles Frederick Worth (who redefined the role of the ready-to-order dressmaker into that of the fashionable artist regularly launching new styles from the opening of his first shop in 1858) and John Galliano (who revived the house of Christian Dior with exuberant excess from 1996 until 2011). Worth's fame saw him recognized as an aesthetic tastemaker. He was even parodied in Emile Zola's 1872 novel, *The Kill*, a vicious dissection of the vulgar mercantilism of Second Empire Parisian society, in which commodity fetishism and the proliferation of surfaces (denoted through architecture, décor, and dress) are combined with sexual voracity, gender indeterminacy, and the venal dynamics of property speculation. The "couturier of genius," the illustrious Worms—a legible caricature of Worth—is satirized as a divinity, whose salon was experienced "with religious emotion."[5] In the novel's closing lines, we are told that Renée, the disillusioned anti-heroine, has died in debt to Worms, leaving her father to pay the couturier's considerable bill. Indeed, Worth's own commercial and personal success was a cause célèbre in his time, enabling him to personify fashion by promoting it as the artistic face of consumption. Through the manipulation of the couturier's personality, a host of myths emerged to bolster the symbolic capital of the fashion industry promoting couture as a minor art form and the couturier as a type of celebrity artist, emblematic of the creative destruction readily associated with modernity.

Visions of Excess

Following an understanding of excess as a form of unproductive expenditure,[6] as a challenge to the rational economy of utility, production, and consumption, one important facet of the myth of the designer-as-artist has been linked to a vision of luxury that is not just concerned with surface and ostentation but also bound up in motifs of decadence, decay, and waste. The designer is therefore figured as a morbid emblem of decline, which is where queerness enters the frame. Cultural historian Christopher Breward links the mid-twentieth-century lineage of stereotypical "tragic queers" to the morbid brand of decadence revived decades later by Alexander McQueen's "dying frenzy"—from his début show in 1993, *Nihilism*, onwards, he took a perverse delight in breakdown, literalized in the Spring/Summer 2004 show *Deliverance*, which was staged around a danse macabre in which the models moved frenetically until gradually slowing down and finally collapsing on the ground. The collection was a transposition of the 1969 film *They Shoot Horses, Don't They?*, directed by Sydney Pollack and adapted from Horace McCoy's 1935 novel, a parable of economic competition charting a Depression-era dance marathon that results in the mental decline and physical collapse of the participants.

Fashion, Breward speculates, "in its entropic nihilism, its innate queerness, seeks failure as a conditional price for success. In the cultural, political, social and economic construction of modern homosexuality it has found a cruel and fatal currency for the playing out of its tragic systems."[7] This is important for assessing the legacy of designers like McQueen and Galliano, whose creative work has been widely read as a form of self-revelation—by critic Judith Thurman, who situates McQueen's heady aesthetic conjoining sex and death within the brutal shadow of AIDS, somewhat reductively as "a form of confessional poetry"[8]—and whose lives have been subjected to scrutiny in recent years to fit the biographical template of rise and fall used to exploit sensational breakdowns, dramatic comebacks, and forms of self-annihilation for narrative pleasure. Dana Thomas's parallel lives of McQueen and Galliano, entitled *Gods and Kings*, scrupulously documents their rise to acclaim but luridly charts their fall as victims of mental illness, substance abuse, and industry pressure. Thomas charts the rise of Galliano at Christian Dior as illustrative of the wider industrial processes of financialization and corporatization, through which designers were hired by the expanding luxury empires to revitalize dormant heritage couture houses: "luxury fashion experienced a seismic shift from the business of creation to the business of hype."[9] The biographer's claim that designers were sacrificed in the name of capitalism is nonetheless debatable, given the evidence she provides of attempts by LVMH/Christian Dior Couture to address Galliano's self-harm and substance abuse prior to the public acts of antisemitic hate-speech in 2011, for which he was fired and prosecuted. In any case, in her sensationalistic version of events, McQueen was professionally driven by an innate fear of decline and failure, the fear that he would go out of fashion. "Several of his friends and assistants told me," Thomas confides, "that McQueen was so driven because he was terrified of the 'the dip': the moment when he believed creators had reached their career pinnacle and started sliding downward."[10]

Lurking beneath the melodramatic imagery of freefall is not only a recurrent schadenfreude in discussions of fame and creativity as being fatalistically doomed one way or another, but also the psychanalytic idea of an unconscious will to fail that is used to describe, in Sigmund Freud's terms, "those wrecked by success."[11] By that, he meant that people can fall mentally ill upon the fulfilment of their wish or satisfaction of an ambition and that success unleashes symptoms of unconscious guilt. As Adam Phillips comments in his discussion of Freud's text, there is "nothing like success to show us that we are not quite who we

FIGURE 9 Designer John Galliano in *High & Low: John Galliano*, directed by Kevin Macdonald, 2023.

think we are."[12] This notion of multiple unconscious selves shaping our actions, in which neurotic patterns of self-destructive behavior frustrate the satisfaction of success, also informs a documentary film about Galliano, aptly titled *High & Low: John Galliano* (2023), directed by Kevin Macdonald, which traces the designer's trajectory through the lens of success and failure as they are manifested through the "high" of personal accomplishment and the "low" of publicized shaming.

Shame, cultural theorist Jacqueline Rose reminds us, is a public affect: it "relies on the art of exposure" and it "requires an audience."[13] It is also a fundamental part of the punitive cult of celebrity, which she defines as a ritual of public humiliation, a shared guilty secret, since we routinely require celebrities "to embody or to carry the weight of the question: who are we meant to be performing to, or what are we doing when performing to an invisible audience?"[14] Macdonald's ambivalent film portrait of Galliano charts his "highs" (in both senses of personal glory and euphoric intoxication) by drawing on footage of his rise to prominence as a young designer in London in the late 1980s and early 1990s through his creative run of collections at the couture houses of Givenchy and Christian Dior, which were fueled by dramatic performance and public scandal (the Dior *Clochard* collection of Autumn/Winter 2000–1, for example, was widely criticized for glamorizing poverty). Galliano's successes are diametrically opposed by the "lows" of alcoholism, grief, work pressure, and feelings of shame—failure in the very visible sense of a public fall-out from an event—following the acts of antisemitic hate-speech for which he was dismissed and then prosecuted in 2011. Indeed, the question of contrition and pardon (how to rehabilitate rather than cancel public figures without necessarily excusing their crimes) motivates Macdonald's inquiry, which is supported by the subject's complex negotiation of remorse (filtered through the Catholic guilt and family abuse of his childhood) and a series of psychological testimonials, according to which the designer is said to have unconsciously killed off his public image through unresolved trauma. The film ends by acknowledging his return to fashion in 2014, when he began a ten-year tenure as creative director at Maison Margiela. Following the 2022 Artisanal show *Cinema Inferno* (a mixed-media blend of performance filmed and live-streamed to a digital audience, the text of which included the line "I'm frightened I won't be forgiven … "), Galliano is shot running frantically up a flight of stairs (destination unknown)—a final image that appears emblematic of the incessant forward-motion of the fashion industry and its troubling promotion of success through the public elevation of the designer.

The Master Narrative

The title of Thomas's biography, *Gods and Kings*, is an obvious reference to the fame of earlier twentieth-century designers like Paul Poiret, known in his time as the King of Fashion. In his 1930 memoir, he acknowledged the influence he exercised over his era. "People have been good enough to say that I exercised a powerful influence over my age, and that I have inspired the whole of my generation … Fashion today needs a new master. It has need of a tyrant to castigate it, and liberate it from its scruples."[15] The enduring legend of the autocratic designer, the dictator of the hemline, was later cultivated by Christian Dior, the first designer to appear on the cover of *Time* magazine in 1953.

The biographical narratives of famous (and, at times, infamous) designers, which often trade in codependent clichés of creativity and notoriety, have been given a new lease of life through the scrutinizing lens of social media. The cult of personality is the required edge to get ahead in fashion in the age of social media with digital impact now taken for granted for the younger generation of creative directors like Olivier Rousteing at Balmain, whose personal feed on Instagram is shoppable with a click-through feature to the brand for his million followers; or Simon Porte at Jacquemus who stages his private life by curating his own feed to enhance the overall brand image. On his IG handle @ jacquemus, he strategically posts intimate shots of himself alongside branded campaign imagery and runway footage. Indeed, today, as Pamela Church Gibson argues in her comprehensive coverage of fashion's preeminent position within the culture of celebrity, "designers themselves are in fact expected to feature in the public domain. The new fashion-literate public wants to know about the *person*, here as in every other sphere."[16] Previously, the prestigious couturiers of Paris fashion such as Cristóbal Balenciaga maintained their mystique through public discretion—an historical precedent challenged by the mediated fame of figures such as Chanel and Dior and subsequently displaced by the advent of 1960s pop culture embodied by Saint Laurent, who was in many ways the first celebrity designer to self-consciously fabricate a mass-media persona—that of the tortured artistic genius—relayed through his public image.

Heralded by Dior as "the master of us all,"[17] the mid-century couturier Balenciaga looms large as a spectral figure over fashion's mythology of authorship. He cultivated his mystique despite despising self-promotion, choosing rather to redefine the couturier "as a builder, not a decorator,"[18] known for sculpting rather than encasing the body. Mary Blume's measured biographical assessment paints a nuanced portrait of a volatile professional with an explosive temperament, including details of rages in the workroom and obsessive behavior. The adulatory tone of much of the commentary on Balenciaga that tends to consolidate his mandarin pose as an "absolutist,"[19] a "perfectionist,"[20] or a "designer's designer,"[21] began during his lifetime despite the tardy recognition of his talents by journalists and critics. As Cecil Beaton observed in 1954, reverentially calling Balenciaga a genius, a reluctance to optimize his talents more commercially through media exposure only consolidated his artistic standing as the "master architect."[22] Despite the mythologizing tendency of such a discourse, it does, however, suggest the productive links between fashion and fiction, between forms of (creative) design and (narrative) storytelling, a leading thread lucratively exploited by the commercial strategies of contemporary brands. As Beaton presciently remarked long before the advent of designer branding, "[i]f one could say that fashion is a serial story that never ends, then the good designers [sic] must invent new plot developments to continue the tale, and all good dressmaking must confirm to the fictional pattern of fashion's evolution and continuation."[23]

FIGURE 10 Actors Daniel Day Lewis and Vicky Krieps in *Phantom Thread*, directed by Paul Thomas Anderson, 2017.

In the fictional world of the romantic period film *Phantom Thread*, directed by Paul Thomas Anderson (2017), actor Daniel Day Lewis plays the distinguished English mid-century couturier Reynolds Woodcock—the pointedly phallic name is intentional—who dresses society ladies and foreign princesses while obsessively micro-managing his fashion house assisted by his curt sister Cyril (Lesley Manville). After having her dismiss one unpromising lover for her sloppy eating habits, Woodcock falls for a much younger waitress Alma (Vicky Krieps), a post-war immigrant, who becomes his muse and lover. Beguiled by Alma, he measures her slim body for a couture gown to transform her into his ideal model. The dramatic premise is that Woodcock is a domineering force embodying an earlier form of toxic masculinity. His power, however, is eroded by Alma's perverse attempt—through Munchausen-by-proxy—to master him by poisoning his food to slow down his professional activity through periods of illness; she thus retaliates by controlling him through physical decline and personal failure. The closing scenes indicate Woodcock's willing submission to Alma's conceit, which combines two parallel strands of failure: the sense of decline, breakdown or an abrupt cessation of normal functioning (as in a power failure) with the more obscure sense that derived from the Latin *fallere* meaning to trick or deceive.

On its release in 2017, *Phantom Thread* also tapped into contemporary sexual politics by igniting popular debate online as to the measure of its critique of toxic male behavior. One critic for *Gay City News* even lambasted Anderson for straightening (or potentially re-closeting) the figure of the mid-century couturier,[24] whereas another for *Feminist Frequency* pleaded the case for the film's pertinent interrogation of hetero-patriarchal structures—the clinical narrative is, after all, framed as Alma's story told as a confession to her doctor.[25] In academic circles, the film has been viewed through the lens of a post-Lacanian psychoanalysis with due diligence to the discipline's own theoretical masters.[26] Such interpretation suits the film's Neo-Freudian staging of neurosis generated by the repression of perverse desire through its narrative deployment of the designer as an obsessional type—Jacques Lacan described the obsessional neurotic as an actor playing his role as if he were already dead.[27] Anderson's representation of creativity would also more broadly appear to embody Lacan's general axiom, according to which "desire has no object. Instead, desire is a constant search for something more. To desire something is to be in a state of perpetual dissatisfaction. Desire is self-perpetuating, with the only object of desire being desire itself."[28] Psychoanalytically, then, desire would therefore seem invariably to lead to failure.

With such apparent attention to the film's psychosexual dynamics, one might well wonder whether it is interested in exploring fashion as such. Why set the story in the specific professional milieu of high fashion and the historical context of postwar London? *Phantom Thread* does nevertheless contain within it a subordinate focus on the labor involved in design by insistently showing the couturier at work and emphasizing the collaborative endeavor backstage as much as the front of house salons of seduction, thereby gesturing to the material as much as the symbolic production of fashion. Day Lewis, credited as co-creator of the film's script, transposed his routine method of diving deep into characterization by learning to sew and contributed to the process of shaping Woodcock's appearance. Yet, while the film is indeed invested in the central metaphor of couture with its insistent preoccupation with measuring, cutting, stitching, and unstitching, it sidesteps a fuller historical interrogation of the mythology of the designer within the society of his time.

Costume designer Mark Bridges imagined Woodcock as an impeccably groomed esthete, one whose work is paradoxically becoming unfashionable; he is stuck as a successful—but second-tier—couturier failing to chime with the changing times. Beyond the shadow of Balenciaga, other more local designers of the period—some celebrated internationally in their time like Norman Hartnell, others less revered like John Cavanagh—would seem more obviously to fit the bill in terms of professional models. Like Woodcock, Hartnell designed for royalty (he was appointed designer for Queen Elizabeth II's coronation in 1953) but acknowledged in his memoirs the

FIGURE 11 Actors Daniel Day Lewis and Vicky Krieps in *Phantom Thread*, directed by Paul Thomas Anderson, 2017.

subordination of London fashion to the monopoly of Paris couture.[29] French houses were then perceived as the "originators of trends"[30] and Paris was more commercially competitive than the impoverished London of the postwar era. Hartnell's template of an upper-class, high-society glamour intended to rival the more prestigious Parisian couture was beginning to show signs of age by the mid-1950s and would later appear increasingly anachronistic opposite the younger, popular boutique trends that emerged through the 1960s.

In his essay examining couture as a form of queer auto/biography, Breward unmasks the ambiguous identity of the mid-century couturier in relation to prevailing discourses of visibility and the policing of non-normative sexuality.[31] Reading the autobiographies of Dior and Hartnell, alongside those of Hardy Amies and Pierre Balmain, he not only reveals the tropes of gossip and revelation as bound up in anxieties around identity, privacy, and publicity—through the negotiation of the closet—but also the sartorial codes of homosexuality represented in the tailored, neo-Edwardian look of such couturiers. Cited as a further influence on *Phantom Thread* and noted for his autocratic manner and volatile personality is the Anglo-American designer Charles James, an important exemplar of fashion's queer history of failure. Indeed, Bridges' costumes for the film are pastiche imitations of James' singular sculptural designs. Described by one biographer as "supremely individualistic and self-promoting,"[32] James' renown was tarnished by a checkered history of bankruptcies and failures in ready-to-wear, culminating in a belated botched collaboration with mass retail. As a coda to *Phantom Thread* and as the ghost of a suppressed alternative story of queerness is this surprising anecdote: in 1954, approaching middle-age, nearly bankrupt and facing decline, James, who was the epitome of the urbane homosexual couturier, married a wealthy, young divorcee some twenty years his junior.

American Fashion Story

On the cover of Michèle Gerber Klein's biography of James, contemporary designer Zac Posen is quoted as describing the subject as a great master of fashion and a pioneer of glamour, going on to suggest how the beauty and drama of his creations were matched by a dark reality—the drama of the designs extending to the drama of his life. Clearly, there is an historical lineage of commercial and individual failure to be traced from James through to designers like Posen or Isaac Mizrahi—an American fashion story in contrast to the dominant European narratives of glamour and success of the emblematic figures of the later twentieth century, which include Yves Saint Laurent, Karl Lagerfeld, Valentino Garavani, and Gianni Versace. As cultural historian Stephen Gundle observes in the case of Versace and others, the fame (and in some cases notoriety) of designers of the period was most often dependent on the public staging of their lifestyles and the narrative elaboration of their private lives. "They manufactured not just clothing but the contexts in which clothes were to be worn." Emerging as key "masters of style,"[33] designers came to embody glamour. The gendering of this history of authorship in fashion is evident from the names of the late twentieth-century designers listed above—the focus on predominantly male designers as media celebrities in their own right (bar a few exceptions such as Donatella Versace, Diane Von Furstenberg, or Vivienne Westwood) illustrates the overall gendered bias of cultural discourses of success and failure.

In her "Notes on Failure," novelist Joyce Carol Oates views success pragmatically as "a compromise between what is desired and what is attained," supported by a collective disavowal of failure: "Though most of us inhabit degrees of failure or the anticipation of it, very few persons are willing to acknowledge it, out of a vague but surely correct sense that it is not altogether American to do so."[34] This point echoes Sandage's thesis on failure being not just the flipside but the actual foundation of the American Dream, underpinning its economic discourse of winners and losers.[35]

In American fashion history, the most immediate example is Roy Halston, whose trajectory of rise and fall through the 1970s and 1980s has suited popular biographical representation: Steven Gaines' account *Simply Halston: The Untold Story* was adapted by showrunner Ryan Murphy into a glossy mini-series staring Ewan McGregor for Netflix in 2021: "American fashion designer Halston skyrockets to fame before his life starts to spin out of control" was the strapline chosen to promote the glitzy story of fame and success. Halston's influence grew through the 1970s as his clean and sexy gowns became de rigueur in New York celebrity nightlife and at the height of his success he sold the business and trademark to a multi-brand corporation that licensed its products the world over. As his star began to wane, he made a multimillion-dollar deal (years before co-branding with mass fashion became the norm) with cheap department store chain JC Penney, which fatally devalued his name, which he then spent years trying to buy back.

Not all designers whose businesses fail or whose careers nosedive necessarily follow this fatalistic template so often exploited as lurid melodrama (the end of the *Halston* series focuses morbidly on his substance abuse, AIDS diagnosis, and subsequent death in 1990).

FIGURE 12 Designer Zac Posen in *House of Z*, directed by Sandy Chronopoulos, 2017.

A more nuanced queer inflection of failure should also include all those designers—often of color—whose careers have been for long neglected by mainstream fashion history, such as Stephen Burrows and Patrick Kelly (1954–1990).[36] Burrows was the first black designer to win a Coty (later replaced by the CFDA) award and Kelly was the first U.S. and POC designer to be invited by the *Chambre Syndicale du Prêt-à-Porter des Couturiers et des Créateurs de Mode* to show in Paris in 1988 and the subject of a retrospective exhibition in 2021.[37]

Notwithstanding these important correctives to the overall whitening of fashion history, it is nevertheless true that some design careers have also come and gone in quite spectacular fashion for more obviously financial reasons. In 2001, the *New York Times* heralded the arrival on the scene of the twenty-year-old Zac Posen under the banner "A Star is Born."[38] Sandy Chronopoulos's documentary film of his trajectory, *House of Z* (2017), tells the story of a designer, who was over-hyped by the press while still a student at Central Saint Martins College of Art and Design in London and whose pink brushed-silk dress became a sensation after it was worn at a party by the socialite Paz de la Huerta.

The film uses conventional testimonials to chart the designer's history—the predictable rise and fall narrative arc—from early recognition by the luxury industry to subsequent commercial implosion under the weight of family discord: by the end of the decade, Posen's extravagance and theatricality no longer suited the consumer dominance of sportswear in U.S. fashion and his attempt to integrate Paris couture was deemed a failure. Following Posen's reinvention as a media personality with appearances as a judge on the reality TV show *Project Runway* for six seasons until 2018, the documentary's release in 2017 was conceived as part of the designer's comeback strategy—hubris in hindsight, given that three years later he was forced to shutter his house. *The New York Times* coverage this time asked what had gone wrong, leading the article with the headline "Even 'Project Runway' Couldn't Save Zac Posen."[39] In 2024, Posen was commercially "reborn," starting a new career as executive vice president of Gap Inc and creative director of the group's (failing brands) Gap, Banana Republic, Athleta, and Old Navy, as well as designing costumes for Ryan Murphy's FX limited series *Feud: Capote vs. The Swans*.

The earlier documentary about Isaac Mizrahi, Douglas Keeve's film *Unzipped* (1995) is, like *House of Z*, a revealing counter-example of the homophobic cliché of the self-loathing queer designer. Keeve's sympathetic portrait captures the excitement involved in producing a collection. A rising star at the time, Mizrahi, whose label subsequently folded, gives a charismatic and hyperbolic performance of the designer at work. The film begins with the failure of his previous collection and ends with the triumph of the memorable show that deconstructed the catwalk by simultaneously unveiling the backstage preparations in real-time through a transparent curtain. *Unzipped* eschews the idealist myth of the creative genius in favor of the subject's grounded nature and ironically camp delivery, which are enhanced by the attention to the centrality of gossip to his professional milieu.

The example of Mizrahi is relevant to a consideration of failure because, in his memoir *IM*, he further queers this story by mobilizing his identity as a gay, Jewish New Yorker to shine a light on his

FIGURE 13 Designer Isaac Mizrahi attends AOL Build Speaker Series for *Project Runway All Stars* at AOL Studios in New York on February 22, 2016 in New York City.

trajectory as a designer.[40] There, he details personal insecurities about weight and sexuality alongside his strong work ethic and innate sense of boredom. His insightful memoir explores personal doubts about making a business work, being engulfed by work and feeling undeserving of acclaim. From the mid-1990s, Mizrahi was backed by the house of Chanel, a surprising move in which the brand experimented by financing a U.S. designer through a ground-up business strategy with no licensing, advertising, or retail stores. The publicity generated by the designer's charming personality was intended to compensate for poor sales figures. Chanel was, in effect, underwriting a failing enterprise and Mizrahi finally shuttered his house in 1998. Despite the blunt front-page headline in *The New York Times*: "Designer Most Likely to Succeed, Doesn't,"[41] he later claimed to have felt relief. He subsequently reinvented himself as an entertainer by diversifying his media brand, appearing in a cameo as himself in the

TV series *Sex and the City* and as a judge on the reality show *Project Runway Allstars*. Alongside his appearances on stage in a one-man cabaret show at the Café Carlyle, Mizrahi also made his Broadway debut in 2022 in a limited run in the musical *Chicago*. He concludes his memoir now defining himself as a "performer, a writer, trapped in the body of a fashion designer."[42]

Not all designers, however, are versatile media entertainers like Posen or Mizrahi; others choose to give up fashion altogether.

After Failure

"THE DESIGNER MIGUEL ADROVER IS DEAD" read a post in September 2017 from the IG handle @migueladroverofficial, a declaration in dramatic capitals intended to signal the Spanish artist's career change rather than his actual demise. Adrover had launched his label in New York in 1999, received the CFDA award for best new designer of the year in 2000, proudly claimed the American way of life as his inspiration in 2001, but "went mercurially from rags to riches and back to rags again in only two years."[43] Showing disdain for limiting design to the purely commercial remit of consumer capitalism, Adrover had cheekily used stamped dollar bills as invitations to his Fall/Winter 2000 show. His début had also included a critical take on creative plagiarism with a Louis Vuitton bag repurposed as a mini-skirt together with overt political statements such as a U.S. flag reworked as a jacket and shorts. His second collection contained a Burberry mac turned inside out and reconstructed as a plaid dress (which led to threats of litigation from the brand) alongside the transformation of deceased writer Quentin Crisp's old mattress into a tailored coat. This repurposing of urban detritus was lauded by critic Cathy Horyn at the time as "less recycling than poetic invention."[44] However, his Afghan-inspired Spring/Summer 2002 collection, shown in New York in 2001 on the eve of 9/11, was retrospectively accused of romanticizing Taliban heritage and even led to an investigation by the CIA. The financial fall-out of the dot-com bubble further compounded the label's precarious existence and led to the Chapter 11 bankruptcy of Adrover's main backer, the short-lived conglomerate Pegasus Apparel Group. By 2004, Guy Trebay reported the designer's "incredible rise and inevitable fall" due to global politics and financial mismanagement, reducing the designer's trajectory to the fatalistic media discourse of failure.[45] Since then, Adrover has transformed into an avant-garde artist based in his native Majorca. In 2022, *WWD* also reported the death of his former pattern-cutter, Peter Hidalgo, who had launched his own label in 2006 but who, despite dressing pop stars Kanye West, Usher, and Nicki Minaj, had struggled to secure lasting financial backing for his brand. Sensationalistic tabloid coverage of the designer's death (under the gleeful headline "Fallen Star") noted that Hidalgo had been temporarily housed in a homeless shelter, also mentioning Adrover's premonitory warning to leave New York and give up fashion.[46]

Giving up, according to Adam Phillips, when in anticipation of an alternative future, "is a sign of the death of a desire."[47] Habitually

FIGURE 14 Designer and artist Miguel Adrover.

thought of as a type of failure, or even a suicidal ideation in more clinical terms, giving up could, in fact, more pragmatically be reconfigured formatively as an openness to reconsideration: both "turning back" and "giving up," Phillips writes, "are reversals of a kind, expressions of doubt about progress and desire, or at least about direction and purpose."[48]

In the context of design, choosing to give up or to opt out is part of the emergence of forms of fashion design after failure. This critical re-positioning of creativity (after failure and after Fashion) is a productive way of designing differently, ambivalently repositioning the designer, in part, outside the industrial norms, business circuits, and discursive framework of the system. Beyond opting out (there are indeed numerous examples of designers with careers after fashion such as Helmut Lang and Martin Margiela in the visual arts or José Levy and Kenzo Takada in interior design), there are also instances of designers whose commercial failure is in fact a productive way of interrogating the boundaries of creativity from the periphery. As an exemplar of this minor practice of fashion, one might consider the trajectory of gifted Belgian designer Olivier Theyksens, positioned on the margins of corporate luxury, whose graceful style mixed with a Gothic romanticism was deemed commercially unviable at the French heritage houses Rochas and Nina Ricci. "I would like to stop global vulgarity," he is quoted as saying in reference to the market-driven model of mega-brands such as Gucci, Saint Laurent, and Balenciaga, where the business of prized accessories trumps the design of semi-bespoke made-to-measure clothing that Theykens was pioneering at Rochas.[49] He became "a cautionary tale about fashion's dangerous slide on the slippery slope of commerce and the inability of money men to support talent and creativity."[50] Despite a stint as creative director at the contemporary U.S. brand Theory in New York between 2010 and 2014, his work now intersects more with curatorial and art practice, situated on the margins of the fashion industry.[51]

In his book *The Success and Failure of Picasso*, art critic John Berger once associated success with assimilation and failure with rejection by noting the number of fine artists who had never achieved the success they deserved. "Nevertheless," he noted, "they are the exception, sometimes because, courageously and intelligently, they have wanted to be so."[52]

Helmut Lang, once a dominant creative force in 1990s minimalist fashion, quit the industry in 2005 due to the commercial decline of his brand and discontent with the Prada Group, which had bought it in 1999 for a hundred million dollars but subsequently deemed it unprofitable. Finding himself in "a state of freefall," according to a report in *The New York Times* titled "Decline and Fall of Helmut Lang," the designer's retreat (or "ejection" in the words of the journalist) followed a familiar pattern in the business of fashion: "designers have long sold control of their labels for cash to grow, then clashed with the new bosses and had to leave."[53] In 2008, Lang, who had become a visual artist based in East Hampton, New York, shredded thousands of pieces salvaged from the near-destruction of his personal archive to make pillar-like sculptures for an installation bearing the provocatively phallic title "Make It Hard"—a pointed commentary on materiality and temporality, in which the re-use of destroyed clothing was repurposed as the basic material of queer art. Indeed, Jack Halberstam mentions the "ethos of resignation to failure, to lack of progress and a particular form of darkness, a negativity really" as a specifically queer aesthetic project.[54] And the larger question of time (and counter-hegemonic queer temporalities) would also point to the type of working model espoused by Azzedine Alaïa, who ignored the imposed seasonal calendar of fashion shows, preferring to present his collections when he was ready, in his own time. This was an artisanal means of opting out of normative commercial fashion time, so as to reject the industrial intensification and technological acceleration of design, which divest brands of creative freedom.[55] Such a rejection of the normative time frame of production and communication also impacts on the public (in-)visibility of the designer.

Martin Margiela provided a template for willingly failing to give the performance of success publicly expected of the fashion designer.

In the documentary *Margiela: In His Own Words* (2019), directed by Reiner Holzemer, one of the industry's prominent entertainers, Jean-Paul Gaultier—whose own media "iconicity" was enshrined in the 1980s by his signature look of peroxide blond hair and *marinière* striped tops—remarks on the extreme discretion and radical anonymity of Margiela, a former assistant who had managed to dodge the expected public self-performance through an invisible twenty-year tenure of his eponymous house from 1988 to 2008. Margiela's elevation to the status of "greatness" was apparent in the retrospective exhibition of his work at the Palais Galliera in Paris in 2018, in the catalogue for which the museum's director Miren Arzalluz compared him favorably with Balenciaga: both designers "profoundly changed the sartorial codes of their respective eras … neither succumbed to the frenetic pace of the industry or to media pressure, preferring to take refuge in an almost heroic discretion … to devote themselves to perfecting their trade."[56] Caroline Evans is, however, more skeptical about Margiela's legacy, commenting that while his shows clearly problematized the idea of the fashion spectacle, "it could equally be argued that Margiela simply traded on a particularly exclusive kind of cultural capital which required insider knowledge of new fashion signs."[57] Evans locates a leading paradox running through his career: known to be critical of the corporate structures of fashion through an "aesthetic of ruination," Margiela's position as a designer, "however oppositional or experimental it might be" remained "locked … into the very capitalist system whose cycles of production and consumption it might be seen to be criticizing."[58]

According to Holzemer's film, Margiela's power lay precisely in his anonymity. Unlike the exposure of other designers of the period, Margiela was indeed conspicuous by his absence from public scrutiny. For some forty-one collections spread over twenty years, he never once appeared on stage or gave press interviews to promote his collections. As evident from the film's focus on testimonial authorship, Margiela remains invisible, providing a voice-over narration of his career, showing only his hands as they unpack his personal archive of ephemera. His anonymity also erased intentional authorial discourse from the promotion of the label: "I don't like the idea of being a celebrity," he comments in voice-over. "Anonymity is very important to me. And it balances me that I can be like everybody else. I always wanted to have my name linked to the product I created not the face I have." He acknowledges invisibility as more than simply a PR strategy; rather, it allowed him a layer of protection as both a professional and individual. All public relations were denied, part of a personal choice to protect himself from the industry. *The Business of Fashion* talked of the designer's cult of invisibility, the press of Margiela as a mystery man, one whose strategy actually fueled more interest in his label from the challenge of an identity (or rather, a personality) withheld. Margiela's deconstruction of authorial origination (which included a "greatest hits" ten-year retrospective of his existing collections in 1999) meant designing collections that would be impactful without the imprint of his own face or body.

Margiela: In His Own Words toys with discourses of authorship by denying the designer's visible presence but simultaneously reiterating the undeniable "greatness" and perennial influence of his designs, thereby falling back on an idealist discourse that mobilizes authorship—however invisible—as a commodity and equates success to renown. After all, Margiela's intention was always for his name to be known. In the final analysis, he assured his heritage through a timely retreat from the industry in the late 2000s, at the very moment of its full transformation into a form of digital entertainment, thereby resisting the rise of online marketing by retiring following the transition from a design house into a lifestyle brand. In 2022, Margiela presented his first solo exhibition of over twenty artworks (comprising installations, sculptures, collages, paintings, and films) at the Lafayette Anticipations art space in Paris; the retrospective rationale for the show was that Margiela had in fact been an artist all along.

FIGURE 15 Under the influence of Margiela: an invisible Demna attends the 2021 Met Gala celebrating *In America: A Lexicon of Fashion at The Metropolitan Museum of Art*, September 13, 2021, New York.

Thus far, we have been deploying the preposition *after* to symbolize a rational choice to quit the fashion industry and move into the exhibition spaces of contemporary visual art. However, we might also want to reconfigure failure as a more formative way of repositioning a space for creatives who remain within the industry.

How might a type of commercial failure in purely capitalist terms actually be formative for a designer?

To what extent is failure a productive way of critiquing consumer capitalism from within?

A CALL TO ACTION

FASHION AFTER FAILURE

The ideology of slowness, which represents a major cultural shift in our time, dispenses with the traditional economic doxa of fashion: it signals the failure of an economic model based entirely on continuous growth.[1] Hazel Clark's framework for rethinking fashion is important for considering the value of failure with regard to ecological questions of sustainability, ethics, labor, and gender. By challenging the inherent notion of novelty in fashion, confronting the industry's over-reliance on image, rethinking fashion as something chosen rather than imposed and highlighting collaborative and cooperative work, which potentially gives more agency to women.[2] This question of gender is indeed essential in defining a new fashion time and generating new fashion practices.

Marine Serre's designs are relevant in this context. A book co-written with anthropologist Marc Abélès, *Re-generation: fashion for the world that comes after*, documents how the initial reception of her collections followed the predictable success story of fashion—a graduate of La Cambre school in Bruxelles in 2016, she won the prestigious LVMH prize in 2017 for her graduation collection, *Radical Call for Love*. Since her debut Fall/Winter 2018 show at Paris Fashion Week, the designer has become associated with a critical type of eco-futurism: technologically forward-thinking, Serre's practice of regeneration involves upcycling and incorporating materials that have no intrinsic value such as bedsheets, old jeans, and recycled fabrics. Her small business operates out of a warehouse in north-east Paris, adjacent to Le Centquatre Paris contemporary public art space. What is interesting about Serre's brand positioning is the contradiction between her emergence as an independent, commercially viable brand (hyped by the media and influencers and worn by stars and celebrities) and her ideological critique of the industry's practices: particularly the futility of the fashion cycles and exhaustion of resources. Seeing clothes as having their own lifespan, she interrogates the function of the designer in an age of ecological apocalypse: "I wondered quite simply what the point was of a designer creating clothes if their production was disconnected from the issues of the apocalyptic world that we inhabit."[3] Serre situates herself as a designer breaking with the traditional values of aestheticization (seen as having failed the planet) to introduce survival and durability as central pillars of her project of re-generation—a twenty-first-century rethink of modernity beyond the historical remnants of fashion's futility and ephemerality. All her collections are named with a critique of the failed ecosystem in mind: her signature apocalyptical vision is encapsulated through offerings titled *Radiation* (Fall/Winter 2019) and *Black Tide* (Spring/Summer 2020). The film for the Spring/Summer 2022 collection, *Ostal 24* (*Ostal* is an Occitan word for house) showed ordinary garments made from upcycled materials and old scarves—the play on words of *fichu* (scarf as a noun, it also means broken as an adjective) emphasizing the parallel investigation into both re-use and failure.

Similarly, the work of the Paris-based couturière Stéphanie Coudert, whose trajectory I evoked briefly in the preface, also offers insight into the business models and operating conditions for emerging designer labels because she failed to position herself as a brand. She showed on the haute couture calendar and in 2014 found an investor who injected capital that enabled her to expand according to the traditional model of global distribution. However, Coudert failed to manage the dual role of entrepreneur and designer. In a round-table discussion at

FIGURE 16 Marine Serre attends the Business of Fashion BoF 500 Class of 2024 during Paris Fashion Week at Shangri-La Hotel Paris, September 28, 2024, Paris, France.

the International Festival of Fashion, Photography and Accessories in Hyères in April 2019, she broached the seemingly embarrassing subject of failure as a designer—an issue that many young designers do not feel comfortable evoking in public. Coudert admitted to having mistakenly confused her creative aspirations as a designer with the simultaneous need to manage a business as a brand. Beginning with a classic distribution model with sales points in Europe and East Asia, her business developed at such a rate that 90 percent of her time was spent managing her brand rather than designing. Scaling back her operation to one studio in Belleville in north-east Paris, where she tailored semi-bespoke ready-to-wear for selected clients, allowed her to maintain control of a modest business while being able to be creative. She defined herself as a creator of made-to-measure clothing; indeed, dress-making is seen as an artisanal practice in the French tradition.[4] Her name disappeared in the transition from Stéphanie Coudert to Service Couture, thereby marking a shift from the person to the activity, from the couturiere to the artisan. However,

FIGURE 17 Stéphanie Coudert Haute Couture Spring/Summer 2015, Paris Fashion Week.

the importance of branded authorship saw the reappearance of the label Maison Coudert, with the opening of a short-lived boutique on the chic left-bank of Paris, which traded in the vintage style of the traditional artisan. This precarious reduction in scale (from fashion-branding to dress-making) also taps into the discourse of slowness as a much broader ideological attempt to rethink fashion critically beyond the prescriptive templates of fame, success, growth, and expansion, traditionally laid down by the industry.

Opting out of the system of corporate fashion branding can therefore be viewed as an oppositional way to maintain independence and balance while accepting the commercial need to survive as a niche business. This is not just a cynical type of repositioning *after* branding but rather the means for a creative to set the terms of their own agenda, which might indeed come down to ideological or political oppositionality, or more personal or professional life choices. If capitalism is therefore viewed pragmatically as a collective fate for those wishing to pursue a fulfilling career in fashion design, then how can they live with it, let alone transform it? How, for example, to make a sustainable or regenerative brand successful in both commercial and ethical terms?

As we conclude our study of failure in fashion, it is worthwhile mentioning that to think about the value of failure does not simply equate to analyzing the fashion system as a background or a context for discussions of individual instances of designer-branded success or failure but rather to offer a "conjunctural" analysis as a call to action, the start of a critical conversation about the commercial and creative culture of fashion today and how we might collectively reimagine it. Rather than argue for one neat or epochal narrative like the "end" of fashion, I choose to follow Lawrence Grossberg's positioning of the interdiscipline of Cultural Studies as an ongoing, open-ended project, "a conversation across many fields, discourses, knowledges and institutions, a conversation one seeks to advance by humbly offering the best contributions one can."[5] Rather than provide a definitive answer to the question of what failure in fashion represents, the approach adopted here has aimed to interrogate the creative and commercial parameters of twenty-first-century fashion to ask what is specific about the current conjuncture that privileges the corporate success stories (and those media narratives that rely on the perverse pleasure taken in the failure of others) over alternative renditions of creative independence, ethical critique, and material regeneration. Failing to adhere to the dictates of the industrial-designer complex as the imposition of a neoliberal quest for fame and fortune would therefore involve breaking the cultural taboo of discussing failure more openly and sharing good practice.

A post on LinkedIn (the emblematic business social media platform for professional networking and self-promotion) by French entrepreneur and ambassador for circular economy, Anaïs Dautais Warmel, describes her personal experience of failure following the closure of her upcycling label, Les Récupérables (The Recoverables), first launched in 2016, which had helped democratize upcycling in France.[6] The label was distributed by wholesalers and sold more than thirty thousand upcycled articles but, despite a turnover of half a million euros and the launch of two stand-alone boutiques, the financial unsustainability of its business model led Dautais Warmel to put the label into receivership in 2022. However, the interlocking dynamic of gender, labor, and precarity in the creative sector is not such a recent phenomenon. Writing over twenty years ago in *Feminist Review*, cultural theorist Angela McRobbie zeroed in on the gendering of creative work in the UK design sector, highlighting a form of "female self-generated work giving rise to collaborative possibilities and co-operation"[7] amidst the surrounding neoliberal discourses of female individualization in the fashion business. As McRobbie trenchantly put it, "staying small contradicts the logic of capitalist enterprise"[8] with its normative definition of success understood in terms of capital investment and logistical expansion into global markets. Despite a passion for creative design and a desire to carve out a rewarding professional career in fashion, of the local female-led brands McRobbie discussed, few remained in business for long. "Who is left in the independent sector?"[9] she asked with dismay.

The difficulties of small labels since then have only been compounded after digital by the crisis in luxury e-commerce and the more recent collapse of wholesale impacting on the solvency of fashion brands. In 2024, *Vogue Business* drew up the growing list, post-pandemic, of failed indie brands that included Mara Hoffman, Calvin Luo, The Vampire's Wife, Victoria/Tomas, and Christopher Kane, addressing how unstable the current economic situation is for independent labels and how near-impossible it is for them to balance their books, let alone thrive.[10] Louis Gabriel Nouchi, founder of the LGN men's ready-to-wear label in Paris, underlines the archaic distribution system that hinders small designers who are overly dependent on wholesale: "being the head of a fashion house now," Nouchi observes, "is not only about designing clothes but creating a whole new system adapted to both sustainable design and today's market."[11]

However, to end on a more optimistic note with a more hopeful instance of design practice after the failure of the fashion system: the documentary *Fashion Reimagined* (2022), directed by Becky Hutner, is a portrait of the British designer Amy Powney, the daughter of environmental activists, who grew up off-grid on a farm in rural Lancashire in North-West England and who trained as a designer at Kingston University. She started as an assistant at the brand Mother of Pearl (a sustainable luxury womenswear label founded by Maia Norman in 2002) and worked her way up to become the brand's creative director and owner. The film traces Powney's efforts to transform the industry by producing an entirely sustainable collection—*No Frills*, launched at the London Fashion Week in September 2018. This ambition represents a call for a more critically reflective design practice for future generations, providing a message of hope rather than despair. After winning the 2017 British Vogue and Council of Fashion Designers annual award of £100,000 (a meager sum to invest in a fashion business these days), Powney decided to use the prize money to make an entirely ecologically and ethically responsible clothing line, one that would represent the antithesis of the traditional aesthetic of glamour in fashion. The aim of the No Frills collection was to use organic materials from a transparent supply chain, which placed social responsibility, respect for animals, and low-ecological impact above cost. Crucially, the collection upended the design process, beginning not with an aesthetic concept but rather with a material question: how to avoid contributing to the waste and harm of industrial production, to the toxic emissions, animal cruelty, intensive farming, plastic mountains, and sweatshop labor practices that plague fashion today? With her product development and brand manager, Chloe Marks, Powney attempted to trace the sources of the wool and cotton used to spin the fabrics for the collection, traveling to Uruguay, Peru, Austria, and Turkey in an effort to disrupt an unsustainable supply chain.

Success, in this instance, is simply the designer's capacity to generate an entirely sustainable collection, nothing more—not success or failure measured according to the commercial criteria of sales, publicity, or appraisal. Nevertheless, the buzz generated by the collection at LFW did enable Powney to reposition the brand

FIGURE 18 Designer Amy Powney in *Fashion Reimagined*, directed by Becky Hutner, 2022.

commercially as a wholly sustainable one—a market positioning now more widely adopted across the sector.

Out of the collapse of an unsustainable system emerges a template for a critical practice of fashion beyond the one-dimensional business paradigm of success and profit. One might indeed interpret *Fashion Reimagined* as documenting the ongoing attempts to overhaul the industry more radically by evacuating design of its neo-capitalist discourse, thereby redefining fashion beyond purely economically quantifiable categories such as the business fail, as well as suggesting more ideologically open-ended ways of making trouble and questioning everything (to paraphrase a T-Shirt slogan once used by fashion designer, eco-warrior, and political agitator Katherine Hamnett, who is also interviewed in the film).

One thing that is striking in the larger political contest around the long-term durability of the fashion industry—if indeed it is to survive at all in its present configuration, which is by no means guaranteed at this point—is the extent to which critical fashion practice is clearly rooted in the longer materialist history of feminism—admittedly an overly white feminism going on the absence of intersectional formations such as black feminism, critical race theory, or queer of color critique in such representations of the industry. However, on balance, given the current ideological, economic, and ecological conjuncture of extremism, collapse, and meltdown, this counts as a progressive call for action none the less.

Fashion Reimagined concludes with a quotation attributed to an overlooked, mid-twentieth-century American designer, Anne Klein, who once said: “Clothes aren’t going to change the world. The women who wear them will.”[12] Dispensing with received notions of success and failure in fashion (a neoliberal mantra that promotes the values of profit, growth, competition, individualism, and celebrity as end goals in themselves) and doing something else altogether might well be an important part of that necessary change.

NOTES

Preface

1 Edith Head with Joe Hyams, *How to Dress for Success* (Random House, 1967).

2 John T. Molloy, *Dress for Success* (Warner Books, 1976).

Chapter 1

1 Sonnet Stanfill and Elisabeth Murray, eds., *Naomi in Fashion* (V&A Publishing, 2024), 160.

2 Tim Edwards, *Fashion in Focus: Concepts, Practices and Politics* (Routledge, 2011), 143.

3 Edwards, *Fashion in Focus*, 143.

4 Scarlett Conlon, "Dior's Kim Jones: 'These jobs are not an easy ride'," *Guardian*, April 6, 2019.

5 Steven Kurutz, "How Marc Jacobs Fell Out of Fashion," *New York Times*, June 2, 2018.

6 Bill Cunningham, *Fashion Climbing: A Memoir with Photographs* (Penguin, 2018); Alicia Drake, *The Beautiful Fall: Fashion, Genius and Glorious Excess in 1970s Paris* (Bloomsbury, 2006).

7 Guy Trebay, "In This Front Row, Downtown Cred," *New York Times*, September 13, 2007.

8 Anja Aronowsky Cronberg, "Editor's Letter," *Vestoj: The Journal of Sartorial Matters* 6 (2015): 7–8.

9 Aronowsky Cronberg, "Editor's Letter," 8.

10 Marjorie Garber, *Loaded Words* (Fordham University Press, 2012), 4–5.

11 Christopher Norris, "Jacques Derrida in Discussion with Christopher Norris," *Deconstruction Omnibus Volume*, ed. A. Papadakis, C. Cooke, and A. Benjamin (Rizzoli, 1989), 71.

12 Norris, "Jacques Derrida in Discussion," 71.

13 Roland Barthes, *Roland Barthes by Roland Barthes*, trans. Richard Howard (University of California Press, 1977), 156.

14 Roland Barthes, *The Neutral: Lecture Course at the Collège de France (1977–1978)*, trans. Rosalind E. Krauss and Denis Hollier (Columbia University Press, 2005), 6.

15 Leo Bersani and Ulysse Dutoit, *Arts of Impoverishment: Beckett, Rothko, Resnais* (Harvard University Press, 1993), 1.

16 Tim Dean, Hal Foster, Kaja Silverman, and Leo Bersani, "A Conversation with Leo Bersani," *October* 82 (1997): 3–16.

17 Leo Bersani and Nicholas Royle, "Beyond Redemption: An Interview with Leo Bersani," *Oxford Literary Review* 20, no. 1/2 (1998): 174.

18 See Danielle Wightman-Stone, "Alexandre Mattiussi's luxury label Ami takes on Chinese investor," *Fashion United*, January 7, 2021.

19 The video ("J'ai lancé ma marque et … c'était un flop") was posted by Léna Situations on her YouTube channel, July 9, 2023.

20 Marisa Meltzer, *Glossy: Ambition, Beauty, and the Inside Story of Emily Weiss's Glossier* (One Signal Publishers/Atria, 2023), 215.

21 See for example Giorgio Armani, *Giorgio Armani Per Amore* (Rizzoli, 2023); Tommy Hilfiger with Peter Knobler, *American Dreamer: My Life in Fashion & Business* (Ballantine Books, 2016).

22 Samuel Beckett, *Worstward Ho* (Grove Press, 1983), 8.

23 Noah Johnson, "Can Yohji Yamamoto Save Fashion from Itself?" *GQ*, April 6, 2023.

24 Yohji Yamamoto, *My Dear Bomb*, text by Yohji Yamamoto and Aï Mitsuda (Ludion, 2010), 107–8.

25 At the start of the century, two seminal texts by fashion historians Rebecca Arnold and Caroline Evans located forms of negativity (imperfection, anxiety, morbidity, trauma, dereliction, and deathliness) at the heart of 1990s designer fashion. See Rebecca Arnold, *Fashion, Desire and Anxiety: Image and Morality in the Twentieth Century* (Rutgers University Press, 2001) and Caroline Evans, *Fashion at the*

Edge: Spectacle, Modernity, and Deathliness (Yale University Press, 2003). More recently, in the introduction to their volume *Fashion and Feeling: The Affective Politics of Dress*, Roberto Filippello and Ilya Parkins ask the following questions: "What does fashion look and feel like in an age dominated by amplified anxiety, isolation, depression, and precarity? How are feelings woven into clothing and mobilized through fashion practices in ways that might sustain living with a sense of ongoing crisis? … And does [fashion] have the potential to help us imagine new lifeworlds which might be reinvigorating? In other words, how is fashion engaging with the 'bad,' the 'good,' and the ambivalent feelings associated with our personal and collective histories, with our troubled political present, and with our imagined future?" Roberto Filippello and Ilya Parkins, eds., *Fashion and Feeling: The Affective Politics of Dress* (Palgrave Macmillan, 2023), 2.

26 Jenny Odell, *Inhabiting the Negative Space* (Harvard University Graduate School of Design and Sternberg Press, 2021), 60. See also Jenny Odell, *How to Do Nothing: Resisting the Attention Economy* (Melville House, 2019).

27 Odell, *Inhabiting the Negative Space*, 62.

28 Judith (Jack) Halberstam, *The Queer Art of Failure* (Duke University Press, 2011).

29 On failure in aesthetics, see Lisa Le Feuvre, ed., 2010. *Failure* (Whitechapel Gallery, 2010); in architecture: Timothy Brittain-Catlin, *Bleak Houses: Disappointment and Failure in Architecture* (MIT Press, 2014); in cultural studies: Colin Feltham, *Failure* (Acumen, 2012), Florian Grandena and Éric Mathieu, eds., *Échecs et vomissements: Réflexions sur l'insuccès comme mode de vie et philosophie* (Éditions Somme toute, 2023); in design: John Sharp and Colleen Macklin, *Iterate: Ten Lessons in Design and Failure* (MIT Press, 2019); in literature: Andrew Asibong and Aude Campmas, eds., *Flaubert, Beckett, NDiaye. The Aesthetics, Emotions and Politics of Failure* (Brill–Rodopi, 2017), Morris Dickstein, "The Authority of Failure," *The American Scholar* 69, no. 2 (2000): 69–81, Pierre-Antoine Pellerin, "L'Art de l'échec: repères historiques et enjeux critiques," *Revue française d'études américaines* 163, no. 2 (2020): 3–30; in media arts: Arjun Appadurai and Neta Alexander, *Failure* (Polity Press, 2020) and Carolyn L. Kane, *High-Tech Trash: Glitch, Noise, and Aesthetic Failure* (University of California Press, 2019); in performance studies: Sara-Jane Bailes, *Performance Theatre and the Aesthetics of Failure*

(Routledge, 2011); in social history: Nicole Antebi, Colin Dickey and Robby Herbst, *Failure!: Experiments in Aesthetic and Social Practices* (Journal of Aesthetics and Protest Press, 2007).

30 For a full elaboration of all these points, see Margaret Werry and Róisín O'Gorman, "The Anatomy of Failure: An Inventory," *Performance Research* 17, no. 1 (2012): 105–10.

31 Alain de Botton, *Status Anxiety* (Hamish Hamilton/Penguin Books, 2004), 4–5.

32 See Joe Moran, *If You Should Fail* (Penguin, 2020), Charles Pépin, *Les Vertus de l'échec* (Allary Éditions, 2016), Kieran Setiya, *Life is Hard: How Philosophy Can Help Us Find Our Way* (Penguin/Random House, 2022).

33 The most comprehensive account to date of the radical call for systemic change is Tansy E. Hoskins, *The Anticapitalist Book of Fashion* (Pluto Press, 2022).

34 Kate Fletcher, *Craft of Use: Post-Growth Fashion* (Routledge, 2016), 59.

35 Fletcher, *Craft of Use*, 269.

36 See Peter McNeil and Giorgio Riello, *Luxury: A Rich History* (Oxford University Press, 2016), 252–88.

37 Halberstam, *The Queer Art of Failure,* 88.

38 Scott A. Sandage, *Born Losers: A History of Failure in America* (Harvard University Press, 2005), 278.

39 Stefano Massini, *The Lehman Trilogy* (HarperVia, 2020).

40 Carolyn Mair, *The Psychology of Fashion* (Routledge, 2018), 27.

41 Imran Amed, "The Fashion System is Creaking. Will It Collapse?" *Business of Fashion*, June 14, 2024.

42 See Adam Geczy and Vicki Karaminas, eds., *The End of Fashion: Clothing and Dress in the Age of Globalization* (Bloomsbury, 2019), 1–4; Valerie Steele, "Fashion Futures," in *The End of Fashion*, ed. Geczy and Karaminas, 5–18; and Caroline Evans, "End Times, Future Visions," in *E/Motion: Fashion in Transition*, MoMu exhibition catalogue (Lannoo Publishers, 2021), 130–45.

43 Lidewij Edelkoort, *Anti_Fashion: A Manifesto for the Next Decade* (Trend Union, 2015).

44 Teri Agins, *The End of Fashion: How Marketing Changed the Clothing Business Forever* (William Morrow and Company, 1999).

45 Georg Simmel, "Fashion," *American Journal of Sociology* 62, no. 6 (1957): 547.

46 Elizabeth Wilson, *Adorned in Dreams: Fashion and Modernity* (Rutgers University Press, 2003), 9–10.

47 Elizabeth Wilson, *The Contradictions of Culture: Cities, Culture, Women* (Sage, 2001), 58.

48 Wilson, *Adorned in Dreams*, 14.

49 Werner Sombart, "Economy and Fashion: A Theoretical Contribution on the Formation of Modern Consumer Demand," in *The Rise of Fashion: A Reader*, ed. Daniel L. Purdy (University of Minnesota Press, 2004), 316.

50 Walter Benjamin, *The Arcades Project*, trans. Howard Eiland and Kevin McLaughlin (Belknap Press, 1999), 894.

51 Ulrich Lehmann, *Fashion and Materialism* (Edinburgh University Press, 2018), 16.

52 Fred Davis, *Fashion, Culture, and Identity* (Chicago University Press, 1992), 159–88.

53 On cultural appropriation in fashion, see Yuniya Kawamura and Jung-Whan Marc de Jong, *Cultural Appropriation in Fashion and Entertainment* (Bloomsbury Visual Arts, 2022) and Khémaïs Ben Lakhdar, *L'Appropriation culturelle. Histoire, domination et création: aux origines d'un pillage occidental* (Stock, 2024).

54 See Nancy Diehl, ed., *The Hidden History of American Fashion: Rediscovering 20th-century Women Designers* (Bloomsbury, 2018) and Elizabeth Way, ed., *Black Designers in American Fashion* (Bloomsbury, 2021).

Chapter 2

1 Anthropologist Ted Polhemus first defined the phenomenon in which consumers sample, recuperate, and aestheticize looks from different subcultures as the supermarket of style. Ted Polhemus, *Street Style: From Sidewalk to Catwalk* (Thames & Hudson, 1994).

2 Sophie Woodward, *Why Women Wear What They Wear* (Bloomsbury, 2007), 3.

3 Woodward, *Why Women Wear What They Wear*, 13. On objectification, see Daniel Miller, *Material Culture and Mass Consumption* (Wiley-Blackwell, 1987).

4 Woodward, *Why Women*, 15.

5 Ibid.

6 Alison Clarke and Daniel Miller, "Fashion and Anxiety," *Fashion Theory* 6, no. 2 (2002): 191.

7 Anthony Giddens, *Modernity and Self-Identity: Self and Society in the Late Modern Age* (Polity Press, 1991), 1.

8 Christopher Breward and Caroline Evans, eds., 2005. *Fashion and Modernity* (Berg, 2005), 2.

9 Ulrich Lehmann, *Tigersprung: Fashion in Modernity* (MIT Press, 2000), 201.

10 Lehmann, *Tigersprung*, xvii.

11 Simmel, "Fashion," 550.

12 Terry Eagleton, *The Ideology of the Aesthetic* (Blackwell, 1990), 317.

13 Walter Benjamin, *Illuminations*, trans. Harry Zohn (Schocken Books, 1969), 261. On the application of Benjamin's concepts, particularly the dialectical image relaying themes and motifs between past and present, see Caroline Evans, *Fashion at the Edge*, 33–5.

14 Philipp Ekardt, *Benjamin on Fashion* (Bloomsbury, 2020), 34.

15 Ekardt, *Benjamin on Fashion*, 43.

16 In his reconstitution of fashion (of written or described clothing) as a system of meaning, semiologist Roland Barthes highlights the arbitrariness of the sign as exempting fashion from time: "Fashion does not evolve, it changes: its lexicon is new each year, like that of a language which always keeps the same system but suddenly and regularly changes the 'currency' of its words" (Roland Barthes, *The Fashion System*, trans. Matthew Ward and Richard Howard (Vintage Books, 2010), 215.) Whereas we talk of mistakes in language, we talk of faults in fashion, Barthes explains, locating fashion's dialectic in the combination of an excessive seriousness with an excessive frivolousness. Barthes describes the time of fashion as a "passion of tenses" (Barthes, *The Fashion System*, 272). The fashionable is thus defined as the rejection of all that preceded it, its own past deemed an

unfashionable countervalue: "every new fashion is a refusal to inherit, a subversion against the oppression of the preceding Fashion; Fashion experiences itself as a Right, the natural right of the present over the past" (Barthes, *The Fashion System*, 272–3).

17 Peter Wollen, "The Concept of Fashion in *The Arcades Project*." *Boundary 2* 30, no. 1 (2003): 138–9.

18 Walter Benjamin, *The Arcades Project*, 70.

19 The epigraphs attributed to Leopardi and Balzac are quoted in Walter Benjamin, *The Arcades Project*, 62.

20 Georg Lukács, *Studies in European Realism* (Grosset & Dunlap, 1964); Peter Brooks, *Realist Vision* (Yale University Press, 2005).

21 Franco Moretti, *The Way of the World*: *The Bildungsroman in European Culture* (Verso, 2000), 134.

22 See Valerie Steele, *Paris Fashion*: *A Cultural History* (Bloomsbury Visual Arts, 2017), 64–8.

23 Honoré de Balzac, *Lost Illusions*, trans. Herbert J. Hunt (Penguin Books, 1971), 160.

24 Honoré de Balzac, *Lost Illusions*, 165.

25 On Balzac's narrative use of decorative and sartorial detail, see Peter Brooks, *Honoré de Balzac* (Oxford University Press, 2022), 60–4.

26 Madison Moore, *Fabulous: The Rise of the Beautiful Eccentric* (Yale University Press, 2018), 36–8.

27 Susan Sontag, *Against Interpretation* (Farrar, Strauss, and Giroux, 1966), 283.

28 Jane Alison and Sinéad McCarthy, eds., *The Vulgar: Fashion Redefined* (Barbican/Koenig Books, 2016), 166.

29 Harriet Walker, *Less is More: Minimalism in Fashion* (Merrell, 2011), 123–37.

30 Georg Simmel, "Fashion," 544.

31 Paul H. Nystrom, *Economics of Fashion* (The Ronald Press Company, 1928), 9.

32 Paul H. Nystrom, *Economics of Fashion*, 9.

33 Robin D. Givhan, "PLUG UGLY: Meet the Plastic Flamingos of Fashion: They're All the Rage," *Washington Post*, May 9, 1996.

34 Miuccia Prada quoted in *Architecture and Ugliness: Anti-Aesthetics and the Ugly in Postmodern Architecture*, eds. Wouter Van Acker and Thomas Mical (Bloomsbury Visual Arts, 2020), 9.

35 Giorgio Agamben, *"What Is an Apparatus?" and Other Essays* (Stanford University Press, 2009), 41.

36 Giorgio Agamben, *"What Is an Apparatus?" and Other Essays*, 48. In their taxonomy of the temporal schema of fashion, Caroline Evans and Alessandra Vaccari also cite Agamben's comments on fashion. See Caroline Evans and Alessandra Vaccari eds., *Time in Fashion* (Bloomsbury, 2020), 3.

37 For an insightful exchange that makes reference to Rei Kawakubo's contesting of Western aesthetic notions of conventional beauty, see Lou Stoppard and Valerie Steele, "Interview: Valerie Steele on 'Ugly' Fashion," *SHOWstudio*, May 12, 2014. On Kawakubo's artful blend of performance and grotesque, see Francesca Granata, 2017. *Experimental Fashion: Performance Art, Carnival and the Grotesque Body* (I.B. Tauris, 2017), 36–53; and on her resignification of clothing through a manifesto and accompanying collection *Not Making Clothing* (Spring/Summer 2014), see Karen de Perthuis, "Breaking the Idea of Clothes: Rei Kawakubo's Fashion Manifesto," *Fashion Theory* 24, no. 5 (2020): 659–77.

38 Mark Cousins, "THE UGLY [part 2]," *AA Files* 29 (1995): 3.

39 For extended discussions of the processes of aestheticization in design and consumer culture, see Daniel Harris, *Cute, Quaint, Hungry and Romantic: The Aesthetics of Consumerism* (Da Capo Press, 2000) and Sianne Ngai, *Our Aesthetic Categories: Zany, Cute, Interesting* (Harvard University Press, 2012). On the definition of kitsch as "unartful," see Jennifer C. Lena, *Entitled: Discriminating Tastes and the Expansion of the Arts* (Princeton University Press, 2019), 151.

40 Bertrand Buffon, *Vulgarité et modernité*, 11.

41 Peter Osborne, *How to Read Marx* (Granta, 2005), 12.

42 Edith Wharton, *The Age of Innocence* (Oxford University Press, 2008), 7.

43 Edith Wharton, *The Age of* Innocence, 11.

44 Pierre Bourdieu, *Distinction: A Social Critique of the Judgement of Taste*, trans. Richard Nice (Routledge, 2010), 490.

45 Thorstein Veblen, *The Theory of the Leisure Class: An Economic Study of Institutions* (B. W. Huebsch, 1899), 131.

46 Cheryl Buckley and Hazel Clark, *Fashion and Everyday Life: London and New York* (Bloomsbury, 2017), 4.

47 Adam Phillips, "The Vulgar" in *The Vulgar: Fashion Redefined*, eds. Jane Alison and Sinéad McCarthy (Barbican/Koenig Books, 2016), 11.

48 Elizabeth Wilson, "The Vulgar: Fashion Redefined," *Fashion Theory* 23, no. 1 (2018): 116.

49 In parallel, in her interpretation of this class-based dynamic Alice Pfeiffer makes a similar point by mobilizing the categories of ugly, kitsch, cheesy, and failed designs as subversive of accepted norms of beauty. See Alice Pfeiffer, *Le Goût du moche* (Flammarion, 2021).

50 See Nick Douglas, "It's Supposed to Look Like Shit: The Internet Ugly Aesthetic," *Journal of Visual Culture* 13, no. 3 (2014): 314–39.

51 Patricia A. Morton, "Camp ugliness: The Case of Charles W. Moore," in *Architecture and Ugliness: Anti-Aesthetics and the Ugly in Postmodern Architecture*, eds. Wouter Van Acker and Thomas Mical (Bloomsbury Visual Arts, 2020), 175.

52 Umberto Eco, *On Ugliness* (Rizzoli, 2011), 394.

53 Eco, *On Ugliness*, 408.

54 Adam Geczy and Vicki Karaminas, *Gaga Aesthetics: Art, Fashion, Popular Culture, and the Up-Ending of Tradition* (Bloomsbury, 2022), 81.

55 Adam Geczy and Vicki Karaminas, *Gaga Aesthetics*, 85.

Chapter 3

1 Richard Dyer, *Stars* (BFI Publishing, 1998), 35.

2 Su Holmes and Sean Redmond, eds., *Framing Celebrity: New Directions in Celebrity Culture* (Routledge, 2006), 288.

3 Leo Braudy, *The Frenzy of Renown: Fame and its History* (Oxford University Press, 1986), 577.

4 Judith Watt, ed., *The Penguin Book of Twentieth-Century Fashion Writing* (Viking/Penguin, 1999), 75.

5 Émile Zola, *The Kill*, trans. Brian Nelson (Oxford World Classics, 2004), 90.

6 See Georges Bataille, *The Accursed Share: An Essay on General Economy: Consumption*, trans. Robert Hurley (Zone Books/Princeton University Press, 1991).

7 Christopher Breward, "Self-Loathing, Ennui and Melancholy: On Tragic Queers and the Failures of Fashion," *Vestoj: The Journal of Sartorial Matters* 6 (2015): 27.

8 Judith Thurman, *A Left-Handed Woman: Essays* (Farrar, Straus and Giroux, 2022), 312.

9 Dana Thomas, *Gods and Kings: The Rise and Fall of Alexander McQueen and John Galliano* (Penguin/Random House, 2015), 209.

10 Dana Thomas, *Gods and Kings*, 291.

11 Sigmund Freud, "Some Character-Types Met within Psycho-Analytic Work," reproduced in Sigmund Freud, *Writings on Art and Literature* (Stanford University Press, 1997), 157–73.

12 Adam Phillips, *On Flirtation* (Faber & Faber, 1994), 48.

13 Jacqueline Rose, *On Not Being Able to Sleep: Psychoanalysis and the Modern World* (Vintage, 2004), 1.

14 Jacqueline Rose, *On Not Being Able to Sleep*, 204–5.

15 Paul Poiret, *En habillant l'époque* (Grasset, 1930), 64–5.

16 Pamela Church Gibson, *Fashion and Celebrity Culture* (Berg, 2012), 186.

17 Mary Blume, *The Master of Us All: Balenciaga, His Workrooms, His World* (Farrar, Strauss and Giroux, 2013), 19.

18 Mary Blume, *The Master of Us All*, 5.

19 Judith Thurman, *Cleopatra's Nose: 39 Varieties of Desire* (Picador, 2007), 204.

20 Bettina Ballard, *In My Fashion* (Éditions Séguier, 2016), 171.

21 Brenda Polan and Roger Tredre, *The Great Fashion Designers: From Chanel to McQueen, the names that made fashion history* (Bloomsbury, 2020), 97.

22 Cecil Beaton, *The Glass of Fashion: A Personal History of Fifty Years of Changing Tastes and the People Who Have Inspired Them* (Rizzoli Ex Libris, 2014), 315.

23 Cecil Beaton, *The Glass of Fashion*, 319.

24 David Ehrenstein, "Heterosexuality's Phantom Stalking," *Gay City News*, December 21, 2017.

25 Anita Sarkeesian, "The Twisted Knots of Power and Control in *Phantom Thread*," *Feminist Frequency*, March 9, 2018.

26 Trent Ludwig, "Phantom Thread: Threading Between Dresses and Debts" in *Knots: Post-Lacanian Psychoanalysis, Literature and Film*, ed. Jean-Michel Rabaté (Routledge, 2020): 164–78.

27 Jacques Lacan, *Le Séminaire, Livre IV. La relation d'objet* (Éditions du Seuil, 1994), 27.

28 Alison Bancroft, *Fashion and Psychoanalysis* (Bloomsbury, 2012), 60.

29 Norman Hartnell, *Silver and Gold: The Autobiography of Norman Hartnell* (V&A Publishing, 2019), 34.

30 Michèle Gerber Klein, *Charles James: Portrait of an Unreasonable Man. Fame, Fashion, Art* (Ex Libris, 2018), 60.

31 Christopher Breward, 2013. "Couture as Queer Auto/Biography," in *A Queer History of Fashion: From the Closet to the Catwalk*, ed. Valerie Steele (Yale University Press, 2013), 117–33.

32 Michèle Gerber Klein, *Charles James: Portrait of an Unreasonable Man*, 9.

33 Stephen Gundle, *Glamour: A History* (Oxford University Press, 2008), 339.

34 Both quotations from Joyce Carol Oates, "Notes on Failure," *The Hudson Review* 35, no. 2 (1982): 232.

35 Scott A. Sandage, *Born Losers: A History of Failure in America* (Harvard University Press, 2005), 278.

36 See Elizabeth Way, ed. *Black Designers in American Fashion* (Bloomsbury, 2021).

37 See Laura L. Camerlengo and Dilys E. Blum, *Patrick Kelly: Runway of Love* (Yale University Press, 2021).

38 Daisy Garnett, "A Star is Born," *New York Times*, February 25, 2001.

39 Vanessa Friedman, "Even 'Project Runway' Couldn't Save Zac Posen," *New York Times*, November 4, 2019.

40 Isaac Mizrahi, *IM: A Memoir* (Flatiron Books, 2019).

41 Constance C.R. White, "Mizrahi, Designer Most Likely to Succeed, Doesn't," *New York Times*, October 2, 1998.

42 Isaac Mizrahi, *IM: A Memoir*, 353.

43 Caroline Evans, *Fashion at the Edge: Spectacle, Modernity, and Deathliness* (Yale University Press, 2003), 260.

44 Cathy Horyn, "Now, Even Rebels Are Looking Ladylike," *New York Times*, February 8, 2000.

45 Guy Trebay, "A Designer's Incredible Rise and Inevitable Fall," *New York Times*, December 7, 2004.

46 G. P. Rodriguez, “FALLEN STAR. Peter Hidalgo dead at 53: Fashion Designer Who Dressed Kanye and Nicki Minaj Dies ‘in Homeless Shelter’,” *The Sun* (U.S. edition), January 30, 2022.

47 Adam Phillips, *On Giving Up* (Hamish Hamilton/Penguin Books, 2024), 4.

48 Adam Phillips, *On Giving Up*, 11.

49 Lynn Hirschberg, “Is There a Place for Olivier Theyskens?” *New York Times*, August 6, 2006.

50 Vanessa Friedman, “Into the Light: The Trajectory of Olivier Theyskens,” in *Olivier Theyskens: She Walks in Beauty*, ed. MoMu Fashion Museum Antwerp (Rizzoli Electa, 2017), 176.

51 Following the monographic exhibition of his career at the MoMu Fashion Museum Antwerp in 2017–18, Theyskens was also invited by Calais Museum of Lace and Fashion (*La Cité de la dentelle et de la mode*) to interpret the institution’s collection alongside his own romantic, Gothic signature style. The *Olivier Theyskens: In praesentia* exhibition ran from June 15, 2019 until January 5, 2020.

52 John Berger, *The Success and Failure of Picasso* (Vintage Books, 1965), 203.

53 Eric Wilson, “Decline and Fall of Helmut Lang,” *New York Times*, May 26, 2005.

54 Judith (Jack) Halberstam, *The Queer Art of Failure*, 96.

55 Azzedine Alaïa with Donatien Grau, *Prendre le temps* (Actes Sud, 2020), 13–18.

56 Miren Arzalluz, “Préface” in *Martin Margiela: Collections Femme 1989-2009* (Palais Galliera/Paris Musées, 2018), 3.

57 Caroline Evans, *Fashion at the Edge*, 42.

58 Ibid., 262.

A Call to Action

1 Hazel Clark, “Slow + Fashion: Women’s Wisdom,” *Fashion Practice* 11, no. 3 (2019): 313.

2 Hazel Clark, “SLOW + FASHION—an Oxymoron—or a Promise for the Future… ?” *Fashion Theory* 12, no. 4 (2008): 428.

3 Marc Abélès with Marine Serre, *Ré-génération: Quelle mode pour le monde d'après?* (Éditions de l'aube, 2022), 40.

4 See Susan Hiner, *Behind the Seams: Women, Fashion, and Work in 19th-century France* (Bloomsbury Visual Arts, 2023).

5 Lawrence Grossberg, "Cultural Studies in search of a method, or looking for conjunctural analysis," *New Formations* 96–7 (2019): 38.

6 Dautais Warmel's LinkedIn post is at: https://fr.linkedin.com/posts/anais-dautais-warmel-6939a030_jai-fermé-ma-boîte-et-il-ma-fallu-1-an-activity-7202202822438793217-lqeD. Going on the numerous supportive comments posted by female users in reply to this post, breaking the taboo of openly discussing failure as an entrepreneur is something to be encouraged.

7 Angela McRobbie, "Fashion Culture, Creative Work, Female Individualization," *Feminist Review* 71 (2002): 52.

8 Angela McRobbie, "Fashion Culture," 55.

9 Ibid., 57.

10 Madeleine Schulz, "The list of failed indie brands is growing: Why it matters," *Vogue Business*, May 21, 2024.

11 Manon Renault, "Face à Trump, la mode en danger ?" *Les Inrockuptibles*, June 9, 2024.

12 The quotation is widely attributed to the fashion designer Anne Klein.

SELECTED FURTHER READING

Abélès, Marc with Marine Serre. *Ré-génération: Quelle mode pour le monde d'après?* Éditions de l'aube, 2022.

Agins, Teri. *The End of Fashion: How Marketing Changed the Clothing Business Forever*. William Morrow and Company, 1999.

Alison, Jane and Sinéad McCarthy, eds. *The Vulgar: Fashion Redefined*. Barbican/Koenig Books, 2016.

Amed, Imran. "The Fashion System Is Creaking. Will It Collapse?" *The Business of Fashion*, June 14, 2024.

Antebi, Nicole, Colin Dickey, and Robby Herbst. *Failure!: Experiments in Aesthetic and Social Practices*. Journal of Aesthetics and Protest Press, 2007.

Appadurai, Arjun, and Neta Alexander. *Failure*. Polity Press, 2020.

Aronowsky Cronberg, Anja. "Editor's Letter," *Vestoj: The Journal of Sartorial Matters* 6 (2015): 7–8.

Balzac, Honoré de. *Lost Illusions*. Translated by Herbert J. Hunt. Penguin Books, 1971.

Benjamin, Walter. *The Arcades Project*. Translated by Howard Eiland and Kevin McLaughlin. Belknap Press, 1999.

Berger, John. *The Success and Failure of Picasso*. Vintage Books, 1965.

Bersani, Leo and Ulysse Dutoit. *Arts of Impoverishment: Beckett, Rothko, Resnais*. Harvard University Press, 1993.

Blanks, Tim. "How to Fix the Fashion System." *The Business of Fashion*, February 8, 2016.

Bourdieu, Pierre. *Distinction: A Social Critique of the Judgement of Taste*. Translated by Richard Nice. Routledge, 2010.

Breward, Christopher. "Self-Loathing, Ennui and Melancholy: On Tragic Queers and the Failures of Fashion." *Vestoj: The Journal of Sartorial Matters* 6 (2015): 23–7.

Buckley, Cheryl and Hazel Clark. *Fashion and Everyday Life: London and New York*, Bloomsbury, 2017.

Buffon, Bertrand. *Vulgarité et modernité*. Gallimard, 2019.
Camerlengo, Laura L. and Dilys E. Blum. *Patrick Kelly: Runway of Love*. Yale University Press, 2021.
Clark, Hazel. "SLOW + FASHION—an Oxymoron—or a Promise for the Future … ?" *Fashion Theory* 12, no. 4 (2008): 427–46.
Clark, Hazel. "Slow + Fashion: Women's Wisdom." *Fashion Practice* 11, no. 3 (2019): 309–27.
Clarke, Alison and Daniel Miller. "Fashion and Anxiety." *Fashion Theory* 6, no. 2 (2002): 191–213.
Collins, Lauren. "The Button-Pushing Impresario of Balenciaga: How Demna engineered the rise—and near-fall—of the luxury fashion house." *New Yorker*, March 20, 2023.
Conlon, Scarlett. "Dior's Kim Jones: 'These jobs are not an easy ride'." *Guardian*, April 6, 2019.
Cousins, Mark. "THE UGLY [part 2]." *AA Files* 29 (1995): 3–6.
Diehl, Nancy, ed. *The Hidden History of American Fashion: Rediscovering 20th-century Women Designers*. Bloomsbury, 2018.
Douglas, Nick. "It's Supposed to Look Like Shit: The Internet Ugly Aesthetic." *Journal of Visual Culture* 13, no. 3 (2014): 314–39.
Drake, Alicia. *The Beautiful Fall: Fashion, Genius and Glorious Excess in 1970s Paris*. Bloomsbury, 2006.
Eco, Umberto. *On Ugliness*. Rizzoli, 2011.
Ekardt, Philipp. *Benjamin on Fashion*. Bloomsbury, 2020.
Evans, Caroline and Alessandra Vaccari, eds. *Time in Fashion*. Bloomsbury, 2020.
Filippello, Roberto and Ilya Parkins, eds. *Fashion and Feeling: The Affective Politics of Dress*. Palgrave Macmillan, 2023.
Fletcher, Kate. *Craft of Use: Post-Growth Fashion*. Routledge, 2016.
Friedman, Vanessa. "Even 'Project Runway' Couldn't Save Zac Posen." *New York Times*, November 4, 2019.
Freud, Sigmund. *Writings on Art and Literature*. Stanford University Press, 1997.
Fury, Alexander. "Meet the Unsung Stars of American Fashion." *Financial Times*, September 6, 2021.
Garnett, Daisy. "A Star is Born." *New York Times*, February 25, 2001.
Geczy, Adam and Vicki Karaminas, eds. *The End of Fashion: Clothing and Dress in the Age of Globalization*. Bloomsbury, 2019.
Geczy, Adam and Vicki Karaminas. *Gaga Aesthetics: Art, Fashion, Popular Culture, and the Up-Ending of Tradition*. Bloomsbury, 2022.
Givhan, Robin D. "PLUG UGLY: Meet the Plastic Flamingos of Fashion: They're All the Rage." *Washington Post*, May 9, 1996.

Halberstam, Judith (Jack). *The Queer Art of Failure*. Duke University Press, 2011.
Hoskins, Tansy E. *The Anticapitalist Book of Fashion*. Pluto Press, 2022.
Johnson, Noah. "Can Yohji Yamamoto Save Fashion from Itself?" *GQ*, April 6, 2023.
Kurutz, Steven. "How Marc Jacobs Fell Out of Fashion." *New York Times*, June 2, 2018.
Le Feuvre, Lisa, ed. *Failure*. Whitechapel Gallery, 2010.
Mair, Carolyn. *The Psychology of Fashion*. Routledge, 2018.
Marriott, Hannah. "Dressing Pretty Is Over: This Is Fashion's Ugly Decade." *Guardian*. June 25, 2024.
McRobbie, Angela. "Fashion Culture, Creative Work, Female Individualization." *Feminist Review* 71 (2002): 52–62.
Meltzer, Marisa. *Glossy: Ambition, Beauty, and the Inside Story of Emily Weiss's Glossier*, One Signal Publishers/Atria, 2023.
Mizrahi, Isaac. *IM: A Memoir*. Flatiron Books, 2019.
Nystrom, Paul H. *Economics of Fashion*. The Ronald Press Company, 1928.
Odell, Jenny. *Inhabiting the Negative Space*. Harvard University Graduate School of Design and Sternberg Press, 2021.
Pfeiffer, Alice. *Le Goût du moche*. Flammarion, 2021.
Phillips, Adam. *On Giving Up*, Hamish Hamilton/Penguin Books, 2024.
Sandage, Scott A. *Born Losers: A History of Failure in America*. Harvard University Press, 2005.
Schulz, Madeleine. "The List of Failed Indie Brands Is Growing: Why It Matters." *Vogue Business*, May 21, 2024.
Sharkey, Lauren. "The Story of Miguel Adrover, 00s Fashion's Unappreciated Enfant Terrible." *Dazed Digital*, February 16, 2018.
Sharp John and Colleen Macklin. *Iterate: Ten Lessons in Design and Failure*. MIT Press, 2019.
Sherman, Lauren. "The Old Fashion System Is Setting New Designers up for Failure." *Business of Fashion*, October 22, 2017.
Simmel, Georg. "Fashion." *American Journal of Sociology* 62, no. 6 (1957): 541–58.
Thomas, Dana. *Gods and Kings: The Rise and Fall of Alexander McQueen and John Galliano*. Penguin/Random House, 2015.
Trebay, Guy. "A Designer's Incredible Rise and Inevitable Fall." *New York Times*, December 7, 2004.
Way, Elizabeth, ed. *Black Designers in American Fashion*. Bloomsbury, 2021.
White, Constance C.R. "Mizrahi, Designer Most Likely to Succeed, Doesn't." *New York Times*, October 2, 1998.

Werry, Margaret and Róisín O'Gorman. "The Anatomy of Failure: An Inventory." *Performance Research* 17, no. 1 (2012): 105–110.
Wilson, Elizabeth. *Adorned in Dreams: Fashion and Modernity*. Rutgers University Press, 2003.
Wilson, Elizabeth. "The Vulgar: Fashion Redefined." *Fashion Theory*, 23, no. 1 (2018): 109–19.
Woodward, Sophie. *Why Women Wear What They Wear*. Bloomsbury, 2007.
Yamamoto, Yohji. *My Dear Bomb*. Ludion, 2010.

IMAGE CREDITS

1. Guy Marineau/Conde Nast via Getty Images.
2. Jesse Armstrong/HBO.
3. Jesse Armstrong/HBO.
4. Darren Star/Netflix.
5. Silvano Mendes.
6. Jamie McCarthy/WireImage via Getty Images.
7. Credit: Kay-Paris Fernandes/WireImage via Getty Images.
8. Kristy Sparow/Getty Images.
9. Kevin Macdonald and Chloe Mamelok.
10. JoAnne Sellar, Paul Thomas Anderson, Megan Ellison, and David Lupi.
11. JoAnne Sellar, Paul Thomas Anderson, Megan Ellison, and David Lupi.
12. Sandy Chronopoulos, Jana Edelbaum, and Rachel Cohen.
13. Laura Cavanaugh/FilmMagic via Getty Images.
14. Brad Barket/WireImage for Henri Bendel via Getty Images.
15. Gilbert Carrasquillo/GC Images via Getty Images.
16. Pascal Le Segretain/Getty Images for The Business of Fashion.
17. Kristy Sparow/Getty Images.
18. Becky Hutner, Lindsay Lowe, and Andrea Van Beuren.

INDEX